The
Strongest
LINK

Forging a Profitable and Enduring Corporate Alliance

Gene Slowinski
Matthew W. Sagal

AMACOM

American Management Association

New York • Atlanta • Brussels • Buenos Aires • Chicago • London • Mexico City
San Francisco • Shanghai • Tokyo • Toronto • Washington, D.C.

Special discounts on bulk quantities of AMACOM books are available to corporations, professional associations, and other organizations. For details, contact Special Sales Department, AMACOM, a division of American Management Association, 1601 Broadway, New York, NY 10019.
Tel.: 212-903-8316. Fax: 212-903-8083.
Web Site: www. amacombooks.org

This publication is designed to provide accurate and authoritative information in regard to the subject matter covered. It is sold with the understanding that the publisher is not engaged in rendering legal, accounting, or other professional service. If legal advice or other expert assistance is required, the services of a competent professional person should be sought.

Alliance Framework® is a registered service mark of Matthew W. Sagal. The Alliance Implementation Program℠, Intellectual Property Disclosure Rules℠, Stakeholder Mapping℠, Decision-Making Analysis℠, Expectation Mapping℠, Conflict Prediction Tool℠, Breakdown Sessions℠, Trust Self-Assessment Tool℠, and Technology Transfer Questions℠ are service marks of Gene Slowinski.

Library of Congress Cataloging-in-Publication Data

Slowinski, Gene, 1952-
  The strongest link : forging a profitable and enduring corporate alliance / Gene Slowinski, Matthew W. Sagal.
    p. cm.
Includes index.
  ISBN 0-8144-0743-9
  1. Strategic alliances (Business) I. Sagal, Matthew W., 1936- II. Title.

  HD69.S8S57 2002
  658'.046—dc21

                           2003005133

Printing number

10 9 8 7 6 5 4 3 2 1

WRITING A BOOK REQUIRES PATIENCE FROM THOSE WHO LIVE WITH THE AUTHORS. WE EXTEND OUR APPRECIATION AND LOVE TO OUR WIVES, KATHY AND REEVA, FOR PUTTING UP WITH US DURING THE YEARLONG WRITING PROCESS. WE ALSO EXTEND OUR THANKS TO OUR FAMILY MEMBERS FOR THEIR CONTINUAL SUPPORT.

C O N T E N T S

PREFACE

It is easy to get caught up in the excitement that surrounds alliances. During the 1990s, American corporations binged on collaborative relationships. Technology-based companies such as Hewlett-Packard, Pfizer, Dow Chemical, and IBM created collaborative R&D alliances to access technology quickly and at lower cost. United Parcel Service and Pepsi-Cola used alliances to access channels and markets that were too costly or too geographically distant to serve efficiently. Internet firms such as Amazon.com and brick-and-mortar companies such as Toys "Я" Us created portfolios of alliances to cope with relentless technological change and to build the foundations of Internet commerce.

The purpose of this book is not to sell the reader on alliances. Quite the contrary, numerous studies show that 70 percent of alliances fail! Rather, our purpose is to introduce a set of tools that will allow the reader to join the successful 30 percent. The high failure rate has two origins: design and implementation. Often, managers with little or no experience are asked to plan and negotiate an extremely complex business structure. When they do not understand the complexities of intellectual property rights, the subtleties of exclusivity, the traps of termination provisions, and the nuances of financial models, these managers craft deals that are fatally flawed. To further complicate matters, once the deal is signed, it is handed off to implementers with little experience in coordinating and integrating the resources of distinctly different organizations.

The Strongest Link provides a practical roadmap to successful alliances, both in design and implementation. Drawing on forty-five years of direct experience, the book describes two proven methodologies that have been adopted by many Fortune 1000 companies, the Alliance Framework and the Alliance Implementation Program.

The Alliance Framework is a rigorous tool for planning, structuring, and negotiating an alliance. When used by both sides in an alliance negotiation, it significantly increases the quality of the outcome and decreases the time needed to reach a mutually acceptable agreement. The Alliance Framework has proven its value over many years in industries such as electronics, telecommunications, pharmaceuticals, chemicals, consumer products, machine tools, energy, and medical devices.

The Alliance Implementation Program is a systematic program that gives alliances the highest probability of success by training participants from both firms in the best practices of collaborative management. Those practices include tools, metrics, and management techniques designed to:

- Support cooperative decision making
- Ensure the coordination of resources across organizational boundaries
- Foster the integration of technical skills between firms

- Provide managers with effective conflict-resolution strategies
- Establish and maintain trust in the relationship

Research Base

The Strongest Link's practical approach to alliance creation and management is based on both firsthand experience and extensive academic research involving companies on four continents. During the past twenty years, Dr. Slowinski's research teams have investigated alliances from every angle. They followed the progress of fifty large company/small company relationships over time. They conducted in-depth interviews with dozens of managers responsible for identifying partners and evaluating their technologies. They surveyed hundreds of managers with direct responsibility for structuring and negotiating alliances. They spent years in the trenches, studying how successful managers interact with their partners on a day-to-day basis.

The strength of this academic research is its link to the business community. Each study was sponsored by a major organization. For example, the Licensing Executives Society opened its doors to help researchers understand how the licensing function affects alliance success and failure. The Industrial Research Institute sponsored many studies with the goal of determining how the technology function can make quantum leaps in effectiveness by combining resources with others. Industry members were active participants on every research team, often outnumbering the academics 5-to-1.

But hands-on experience and years of academic research cannot address all of the complexities found in alliance relationships. To truly understand alliances the authors actively searched for insights from other fields. What do psychologists tell us about managing interfirm relationships? How can anthropologists help managers understand cultural integration? What can marriage counselors teach us about building strong interpersonal relationships in a cross-company alliance? This book is enhanced by all of these perspectives.

How to Use This Book

Creating and managing strategic alliances is an art, but one that can be approached through the use of proven management tools. This book will provide alliance managers and their teams with an understanding of those tools, as well as examples of using the tools in specific situations. But a few words of caution: Alliances are remarkably diverse structures. The reader is not encouraged to create and manage an alliance based solely on the information in this book. Although the tools in this book have been used in hundreds of alliances, the details of their use vary widely. Every deal is different, and managers have differing styles. While we will explain the process and each tool in concrete terms, the reader should understand that the tools must be adjusted to each situation.

Managers must be guided by experienced intellectual property and contract lawyers, and they should use corporate resources such as business development specialists, finance experts, and tax advisers. These experts will assist in identifying and resolving issues beyond the scope of this book, such as valuation of intangible assets, determination of royalty rates, and creation of contract language.

Just as the use of the tools must be adapted to each alliance situation, people's roles will depend on the size and structure of the firm, and the scope of the alliance. For example, we use the term *senior manager* to characterize either the Planning and Negotiating Team Leader or the alliance Operating Manager (i.e., the person who leads an Implementation Team). We use the term *top manager* to characterize a higher-ranking person who oversees either team and has decision-making authority at the higher executive levels of the firm. Examples of top managers are the executive to whom a Planning and Negotiating Team Leader reports, or the person assuming the role of Alliance Executive during implementation. In a small firm, the alliance Operating Manager and the Alliance Executive might be the same person. In a large firm engaged in an alliance of moderate scope, there might be several management levels between these two roles. As we discuss alliance organizing principles, such as team membership and functions and decision making in the firm, readers must adapt these principles to the size, management structure, and style of their own organization.

The best way to use this book is to share it internally with all key stakeholders and externally with prospective alliance partners. The goal is to come to consensus on the tools and techniques that will maximize performance.

Alliances are revolutionary organizational structures that cannot be avoided or ignored. The economic and organizational forces stemming from these relationships are profound. Those firms most active in alliances are engaged in multiple relationships, forming a portfolio affecting many aspects of the firm's business. Well-thought-out alliance portfolios, tightly linked to corporate strategy, emerge as independent sources of competitive advantage for the firm. Haphazard alliance formation is akin to a trip into Dr. Frankenstein's laboratory. Once the firm has created a critical mass of deals, the portfolio takes on a life of its own. That portfolio can lead to some unpleasant places.

Most books are designed to help managers think differently. This book is designed to help managers act differently. The following pages are a call to action, an open letter to our friends in industry who are determined to make alliance creation and implementation a core competency of the firm.

Industries are being redefined by a wide variety of alliances. While there is much talk in the executive suite about becoming the "partner of choice," few firms take the required action of devoting significant resources to build an alliance infrastructure. That infrastructure is needed to support the entire portfolio of co-promotion deals, licensing agreements, collaborative R&D relationships, and dozens of other relationships quietly reshaping the firm. Alliances were once thought of as something a firm *does*. Those days are over. Alliances define what the firm is, and this new perspective is transforming the competitive landscape in fundamental ways.

The remainder of this book is our contribution to your understanding of alliance management, from conception through implementation. The emphasis is on practical tools at every stage of an alliance. We use many examples of actual alliances to illustrate specific issues and the application of the tools.

Part 1 covers the alliance creation process, focusing on the Alliance Framework as the central tool. Chapter 1 begins with an overview of that tool, while Chapters 2–8 describe each step in the Alliance Framework process and the issues that can be resolved through its use.

Part 2 addresses alliance implementation. Chapters 9 and 10 describe the twelve tools of the Alliance Implementation Program. These tools are used to create and maintain productive working relationships between alliance partners. Chapter 11 covers alliance management and measurement systems, while Chapter 12 discusses commonly encountered cultural issues and how they can be handled.

Acknowledgments

Although this book is the result of forty-five years of combined alliance experience, the authors are learning every day. We extend our appreciation to our clients and colleagues for their insights as they help us weave our way through the complex world of alliances. They have shared their failures and their successes, and the learnings that come from each.

An endeavor of this magnitude is the result of contributions from many people. We want to thank the following individuals who provided valuable comments on portions of the manuscript: Wayne Simmons and Laura Silva of Velocys; Harold Hoeschen of Agere Systems; Kazuhiro Endo of NEC Electronics Corporation; Tom Finn and David McCamey of Procter & Gamble Pharmaceuticals; John Tao and Merrill Brenner of Air Products and Chemicals; Judy Sheft of the New Jersey Institute of Technology; and Professor Carter Daniel of the Faculty of Management at Rutgers University. We would like to extend a special thank-you to Kathy

Slowinski for reading and commenting on every chapter—over and over again.

The authors would like to thank Adrienne Hickey and AMACOM for taking on this project, as well as Rutgers University and the Federal EDA, University Center Program for their invaluable support. We wish to thank the following companies who gave us permission to describe their alliance activities: Battelle Memorial Institute, Velocys, New Community Corporation, Waldemar S. Nelson & Company, W. H. Linder and Associates Inc., Agere Systems, NEC Electronics Corporation, Procter & Gamble Pharmaceuticals, and Air Products and Chemicals, Inc. In addition, we thank Windhover Information Inc. and the Industrial Research Institute for allowing us to excerpt information from articles in their journals.

We would like to further acknowledge Christina McLaughlin and Karen Brogno for their efforts at organizing and editing the manuscript, as well as Dr. Alden S. Bean of the Center for Innovation Management Studies at North Carolina State University; Dr. George Farris of Rutgers University; and David Jones and Dr. Frank Hull for their support over the years.

GENE SLOWINSKI AND
MATTHEW W. SAGAL
June 2003

PART 1

PLANNING AND NEGOTIATING THE ALLIANCE

CHAPTER 1

THE ALLIANCE FRAMEWORK®

The Nasca Lines of Peru are a wonder of archaeology. Ancient peoples drew huge figures on the desert floor: pictures of a condor with a wingspan of more than 130 meters or a lizard 180 meters long. These figures are hidden to anyone walking in the desert because a walker only sees insignificant dusty trails and lines of stone. It is only when one flies over the desert at 10,000 feet that the figures take form and the artistry of the ancient people develops meaning.

This chapter is your flight to 10,000 feet. By looking down at the Alliance Framework and understanding how it deals with the fundamental requirements for planning and negotiating alliances, you will understand how the detailed case studies in the following chapters relate to the entire alliance formation process.

What Is an Alliance?

The term *alliance* is confusing to most executives. There is no legal definition. There is not even an agreed-upon definition among practitioners. This leads to confusion as businessmen and women use the term to describe everything from a straightforward vendor/customer purchase agreement to a global R&D, manufacturing, and marketing relationship across a broad product scope.

This book adopts a broad definition because the same disciplined approach should be used regardless of the type of alliance, scope, or complexity. The definition includes four components that differentiate alliances from the more traditional methods of transacting business. An alliance is a business relationship in which two or more independent firms:

1. Work cooperatively on a specific project that is clearly bounded in terms of activity, geography, product, process, and time.

2. Retain an agreed-on level of flexibility. While each firm makes specific commitments to each other within the scope of the alliance, each can work independently of the other on projects outside the alliance.

3. Share in rewards and risks of the project, which may go beyond measurable financial returns to include new intellectual property, skill sets, opportunity costs, and market position.

4. Commit resources to the relationship to accomplish the objectives of the alliance.

The definition covers a broad range of complexity, from an agreement between a manufacturer and a local distributor to a global megadeal. It includes joint ventures as a special type of alliance, in which the alliance partners create a new entity to achieve their mutual objectives. We believe it is a mistake to get caught up in semantics when thinking about alliances. The question is not "Is this an alliance?" The question is, "Can the tools of alliance creation and management help build a strong relationship between two or more firms?" In our experience, the tools outlined in this book are applicable to a wide range of situations, both inside and outside a company. In fact, some of the most attractive opportunities are "internal alliances" between key units of the same firm, such as between R&D and marketing, or between design engineering and manufacturing.

The Definition of Success in Alliance Planning and Negotiating

Before discussing the fundamental requirements for success in planning and negotiating, and how the Alliance Framework meets those requirements, it is important to define "success." Why? Success can have two possible meanings. The first is quite ordinary: The partners reach a mutually acceptable alliance contract that achieves both firms' strategic objectives. The second possibility is less obvious, but equally important: Both sides quickly determine that an alliance should not happen, and part as friends.

Successful alliance executives know the value of the second meaning. When alliance partners spend months in fruitless negotiations, they waste time, money, and energy. When the negotiators finally realize they have reached an impasse, they part as enemies. Each believes the other could have moved the process forward more rapidly, avoiding a waste of valuable time and resources. Potential partners must get to a mutually acceptable deal or stop negotiations—quickly! This is fundamental to successful negotiations. When firms rapidly discover they cannot agree on terms, they should part friends and redirect their efforts to more promising opportunities.

Three Fundamental Requirements of Success

The fundamental requirements for successful planning and negotiation are easy to talk about but difficult to put into practice. Although these three requirements are important in internal alliances, they take on new levels of meaning when working with an external partner:

1. Both firms must clearly understand their own business strategic plan and the ties between that plan and the potential alliance.

2. Both firms must reveal that strategic plan clearly and honestly to the other party.

3. Both must agree on alliance intentions, commitments, rights, and limitations that satisfy the strategic plans of both firms.

Linking the Alliance to the Business Strategic Plan

Why is the first requirement difficult? Why is it so difficult to link alliance formation to strategy? The answer provides insight into why 70 percent of alliances fail.

What is your firm's ability to meet each requirement for success? Can you evaluate a prospective partner's ability to meet each requirement?

Linking alliances to strategy requires that strategy be defined in sufficient detail to guide the planners' thinking. There is a wide discrepancy in firms' ability to define strategy. At one extreme, some firms (or business units within firms) do not have a strategy. They have fuzzy statements about becoming number one in their markets and achieving double-digit growth, but that's true of most companies. If the corporate strategy statement is equally valid for the local gas station, there is no strategy.

At the other extreme, some firms develop excruciatingly detailed strategic plans, sometimes a whole shelf full of them in tastefully designed binders. They have one-year, two-year, five-year, and ten-year plans. Business units have R&D plans, marketing and sales plans, product plans, manufacturing plans, and organizational plans. Most companies fall somewhere in between. The challenge is to translate those plans into clearly defined criteria that identify partners and opportunities.

Another complication is linking the goals and objectives of the alliance to the strategy of *both* organizations. The traditional "do it yourself" style of American management encourages myopic managers. Few understand the implications of the alliance from the partner's perspective. For example, one major tire manufacture created two alliances. The first was with a tire-recycling firm. That alliance was extraordinarily successful because disposing of used tires is a key concern of both alliance partners. The second alliance was with a biotechnology company. The tire manufacture wanted to gain a "window on technology" and understand how biotechnology may impact its business. As you might expect, that alliance went away quickly. Biotechnology is peripheral to the tire business. Assignment to that alliance was like being sentenced to organizational Siberia.   The alliance was doomed from the start because it was not core to the needs of both the tire manufacturer and the biotechnology firm.

How does your firm assess the partner's strategy and its fit to the alliance?

Never underestimate the power of enthusiasm to decouple an alliance from strategy. "Deal fever" is a syndrome that affects both managers new to alliances and those with significant experience who should know better. The best way to describe the symptoms is to say that the deal takes on a life of its own. Executives succumb to the allure of multimillion-dollar payoffs, meetings in expensive restaurants, and the general euphoria of the moment. When disconnects with strategy appear during negotiations, these managers are reluctant to tell the CEO that the big deal already discussed with the Board is flawed. Issues such as the link to strategy and business fundamentals are crushed in a stampede to sign the agreement. How do you know when someone is cured of deal fever? They have the ability to accurately assess a particular deal, conclude that the deal conflicts with strategy, and walk away. The Alliance Framework is a tool that helps managers do exactly that.

Sometimes poorly-thought-out alliance portfolios result from the combination of large egos and misguided reward systems. In one chemical company, a new vice president of business development was hired to "do deals." He signed thirty-two alliance contracts in one year. None were aligned with strategy, none were with first-rate partners, and only a few had clearly defined goals. Why did he do these deals? His bonus was based on the number of alliances created, rather than the quality of the deals.

The effect on the corporation was devastating. Each one of the thirty-two alliances obligated the company to the partners in disadvantageous ways. The accumulated impact of multiple relationships decreased the firm's ability to react to its business environment. Shortly thereafter, the chemical company was put up for sale. (Thirty-two nonstrategic alliances were not the only reason investors were unhappy, but they didn't help the situation.)

The importance of linking the alliance to the strategy of both partners cannot be overemphasized. The world changes at an uncomfortably fast pace. Technological breakthroughs, government regulations, competitive threats, and customer demands fluctuate in unpredictable ways. When the alliance is linked to the strategy of both firms, shifts in the business environment will tend to affect both partners in roughly the same way. Their response will lead both of them in the same direction. It's a bit like two sailboats moving along the same course. When the wind shifts direction, they adjust their sails together to stay on course. Not so when the alliance is more strategic to one partner than the other. Any change in the business environment may benefit one partner and disadvantage the other. This common situation is a fundamental reason for alliance failure. The disadvantaged partner loses interest and shifts resources to more attractive opportunities.

Consider your firm's most prominent alliance, then ask yourself: Is the alliance more important to us than them? More important to them? Equally important to both parties? What are the consequences of the answer?

Path Dependence: The Long-Term Impact of Alliance Formation. The promise and power of alliances is to create new opportunities by joining forces. But there are two sides to that coin. Joining forces can limit a firm's degrees-of-freedom, send it down the wrong trail, or force it to miss an opportunity that might have been available absent a partner. Path dependence is a concept that helps explain how companies lose control of their long-term strategy through alliances. In its simplest form, path dependence states that once we ("we" can be a person, a company, an industry, a society) take one or two or three steps down a path, it becomes difficult to change paths. Everyone has an intuitive understanding of path dependence from personal experience. A commonly used historical example is the standard layout of letters (QWER-TY) on a keyboard. It was originally designed to slow down a typist and avoid jams in early mechanical typewriters. Although mechanical typewriters have long been replaced by computers with their keyboards, we are all still living with that layout today. Efforts to introduce more efficient keyboard layouts have been stymied by the existing installed base and the difficulties of retraining millions of keyboard users.

In alliance terms, once a firm forms one, or two, or three alliances, the company quickly becomes constrained. It loses flexibility as contract terms define where and how resources can be spent, intellectual property provisions limit the use of intellectual assets, and product and/or geographic boundaries direct how the firm will address specific markets. Strategic directions that a firm might take later are foreclosed, and subsequent emerging opportunities are blocked. It is difficult to react quickly to a changing market while tethered to one, two, or fifty partners.

Path Dependence in Alliances: Contractual Constraints.
Path dependence takes two forms, one obvious, the other not so obvious. Let's start with the obvious: the alliance contract. Alliance partners are bound in ways that are carefully spelled out (or should be!) in the alliance contract. That contract may contain provisions that prevent the firm from working with other attractive partners (exclusivity provisions) and make it difficult to escape the alliance and work with a more attractive partner (termination provisions). The contract may require that changes in technical or marketplace objectives be agreed upon between the partners. In short, once a contract is in place, it is difficult to choose a new path, even when the new path is more attractive.

Path Dependence in Alliances: Marketplace Reactions.
The other source of path dependence in alliances is sub-
tler but potentially more powerful. When competitors,
vendors, and customers see an alliance announcement,
they may react in ways that foreclose future opportunities
for one or both partners. A competitor might counter the
strategic move by forming its own alliance. An important
customer might react negatively and find a new supplier.
The marketplace reaction may be based only partly on
facts, since other marketplace participants have not read

THE POSITIVE SIDE OF PATH DEPENDENCE

Path dependence can lead to unanticipated opportunities as well. Here is an example where the customers
saw possibilities in the relationship that were not even
contemplated by the partners. Waldemar S. Nelson &
Company, Inc. and W. H. Linder and Associates, Inc.
compete against one another to provide sophisticated
engineering, design, and project management services
to the offshore oil and gas industry. More important,
they do it in the deep ocean, the most hostile physical
environment on earth. They had no intention of forming an alliance, but a major customer did. The customer realized that if the competitors formed the
Deepwater Consulting Alliance the complementary
expertise of both would be brought to bear on some
very complex challenges. The alliance was quickly successful. It expanded from one project to over a dozen
projects and is still growing. Customers find the combination of the two firms so powerful they see the
alliance as only one "firm." Those same customers continue to encourage the competitors into cooperating
on projects and technologies that neither considered
possible at the start of the relationship.

the alliance contract. They "reinvent" the deal in terms that fit their mind-set about the alliance partners and their perception about the alliance's potential long-term intent.

The "Three Alliances in One" Problem. Beyond path dependence, there is another "understand your own business strategic plan" problem. Simply put, alliances are really three relationships in one. The obvious relationship is the external alliance between the two companies. The two hidden relationships are the internal alliances inside each firm. These internal alliances provide critical resources at critical times to the external alliance. If the two companies are going to achieve their mutual objectives, all three alliances must be planned and negotiated in parallel. Figure 1-1 illustrates this "three alliances in one" idea. In both Company A and Company B, marketing, R&D, and manufacturing have to play multiple roles. Each has to shift resources from internal projects and refocus them on the external alliance. Each has to coordinate its efforts with other internal groups, and each has to

Figure 1-1. Alliances are three relationships in one.

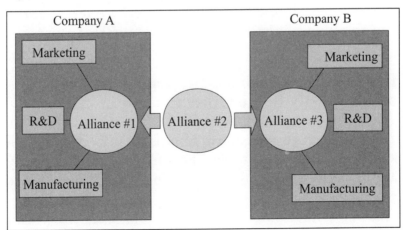

integrate its efforts with groups in the partner firm. The effectiveness of every alliance depends on the ability of both firms to plan and execute all three alliances simultaneously.

The internal alliances are often the most difficult to develop. Achieving internal alignment does not come easily unless the firm has an effective process for exposing and resolving internal differences. Without such a process, negotiators face uncertainty, delay, and loss of credibility as they try to resolve disagreements at home without showing the other side there is a problem. Even worse, unresolved internal disagreements blossom during implementation. The partner quickly realizes that internal groups have different views of the external alliance. As one executive put it, "Managing an alliance with our partner is like dating an octopus. Two arms are hugging you, two arms are strangling you, and no one knows what the other four arms are up to."

Another executive said, "My partner company suffers from multiple personality disorder. Each group in their internal alliance views the relationship from the vantage point of its own narrow interests. When I speak to the marketing group I get one story, the research group another story. I quickly learned that each internal group had an alliance in mind. It was just a different alliance!"

Revealing the Business Strategic Plan Clearly and Honestly to the Other Party

The second requirement for success in alliance planning and negotiating is to reveal the business strategy clearly and honestly to the other party. There are many reasons people are secretive during negotiations. The most important one is that no one knows if the alliance will occur.

Experienced negotiators do not want to reveal too much about their own firm's strategy, intent, and intellectual property position, or get overexposed to their partner's intellectual property. Overexposure is a real risk. When one firm is completely open with another and the alliance does not occur, there is always a question about how the disclosed information will be used. For example, if one firm describes its marketing strategy during a failed alliance negotiation and sees the potential partner using a similar strategy, there are legitimate questions about where, and when, the potential partner developed the strategy. An important aspect of the art of alliance negotiation is the ability to strike a balance between sharing sensitive information and protecting both firms should the deal fall through.

Openness in early discussions also flies in the face of normal negotiating tactics. Negotiators are reluctant to discuss a weakness in their position because it strengthens the hand of the other side. The customary technique is to withhold information that could hurt your firm, emphasize information that helps it, and hope that the partner never figures out which is which. Finally, a certain level of interpersonal trust is needed before each side can be open with the other. When the negotiators do not know each other on a personal level, it is difficult to share sensitive information.

These problems cannot be solved by exhortations to "be open." Negotiators need a process that systematically encourages the appropriate level of openness while moving the process along quickly. The Alliance Framework does that while helping both sides meet the third requirement for success.

Agreeing on Alliance Intentions, Commitments, Rights, and Limitations

The third requirement for success is that both companies must agree on alliance intentions, commitments, rights, and limitations that satisfy the strategic plans of both firms. Coming to agreement requires prospective partners to discuss a broad range of issues impacting the alliance. Some issues are fun to discuss; others are not. Consider an alliance negotiation between a firm with a new product and another firm with a channel to market. If one side says, "It will take two years to get to $75 million in sales," and the other side says, "It will take four years," that's fun to negotiate. Each side looks smart as it makes pithy statements about the marketplace and shows off its analytical ability.

Other issues are not so much fun to negotiate. Suppose the marketing partner says, "In the event another company develops a better product, I want the right to terminate our alliance and form a relationship with the other company. I also intend to take everything we jointly learned about the market into that new relationship and compete against you." That's not so much fun.

Inexperienced negotiators dig themselves into a hole when they spend months discussing the "fun issues" and leave the rest for the end. When the "not so much fun" issues finally surface, it is difficult for the negotiators to walk away. In a very real sense, the deal has taken on a life of its own. Both firms have devoted significant time and major resources to the negotiation. Both negotiators have raised the expectations of top corporate management to extraordinary levels.

This situation leaves the negotiators in a difficult position. When sunk costs are high and top corporate management expectations are even higher, each negotiator has a personal investment in seeing the deal close. This predicament leads to bad deals. The voices in the negotiators' heads say, "It may not be the best deal in the world but the implementers will fix it." This syndrome is called "deal fever." The negotiators, and top managers, are over-committed personally and simply cannot walk away.

———

During your last negotiation, did the partner bring up a threatening issue at the last minute? How many months of effort would have been saved if you had known about that issue early in the negotiation? How difficult was it to tell top management about this "new" development? Did you do the deal anyway?

———

The Alliance Framework: What Is It?

First, let's clarify what the Alliance Framework is not. The Alliance Framework is *not* a step-by-step checklist or a series of fill-in-the-blank forms. Alliances are far too complex for such simple tools. Rather, the Alliance Framework is both a disciplined process and an iterated document. The disciplined process deals with the "three alliances in one" problem by enabling the rapid creation of both internal alliances and the interfirm alliance. Using the Alliance Framework process, you will create a document that describes the alliance in terms of specific elements, with each element describing an important aspect of the alliance. The elements can be thought of as chapter headings in a document that clearly describes the business intents of the partners. As internal consensus is developed and as the alliance is negotiated between the partners, the document is iterated (version 1.0, version 2.0, etc.) to accurately describe the alliance as it takes shape.

We use the same term "Alliance Framework" for the disciplined process and for the iterated document for an important reason: The process and the document are linked. The process is used to create the document. In turn, the document is used to move the process forward. If agreement is reached, the end results are internal consensus among all of the partners' stakeholders, a clear understanding of the alliance among people on both sides, and a final alliance agreement that accurately captures the terms of the deal. If agreement isn't possible, the end result is a quick parting as friends.

It is common for people new to the Alliance Framework to confuse it with a term sheet. There are major differences. Both a term sheet and an Alliance Framework document contain statements describing an alliance as a step toward drafting a definitive agreement between the partners. However, the Alliance Framework is both a document and a process to create and iterate that document within both firms. The elements of an Alliance Framework are designed to enable effective selection of the most likely partner and rapid convergence to a common understanding of all key aspects of the alliance. As a rule, term sheets are incomplete. They miss important aspects of the deal or create misunderstandings between, or within, the parties by using a few sentences to describe complex concepts. The Alliance Framework is complete and rigorous in its descriptions of the deal.

To explain the Alliance Framework in concrete

terms, we will use a stepwise, "recipe-like" description. In actual practice, the Alliance Framework is modified to fit the circumstances of a particular alliance and the management styles of both firms. The next few chapters will provide examples of that flexibility. Since the Alliance Framework's effectiveness increases with experience, reading this book alone won't make an executive an expert. The reader is strongly encouraged to employ experienced business development and legal help during the creation of any alliance contract.

Alliance Framework Elements

While a detailed explanation of each element will be given in Chapters 3 and 8, the following is a typical list of elements. Remember, each element becomes a chapter heading in the Alliance Framework document.

- Business Plan Summary
- Objectives
   1. Ours
   2. Theirs
- Roles
   1. Ours
   2. Theirs
- Overall Resources
   1. Ours
   2. Theirs
- Boundaries
- Market Model

- Strategic Exclusivity
- Intersections
- Detailed Objectives
- Detailed Resources
- Financial Pie-Split
- Intellectual Property
- Working Process and Governance
- Term and Termination

For example, the Roles element specifies the responsibilities of each party during alliance implementation. The Financial Pie-Split element allocates financial rewards and risks. The Term and Termination element specifies how the parties can exit the alliance. While each element is unique, the elements are also interdependent. If the team decides to change its position on one element, they often have to adjust their position on other elements as well. For example, under certain circumstances a company may want the right to drop its partner's product and replace it with a competitive product. That position will be reflected in the Strategic Exclusivity, Intellectual Property, Financial Pie-Split, and Term and Termination elements. Every alliance must have the elements listed. Some alliances have additional elements to reflect industry or marketplace characteristics. For example, pharmaceutical alliances usually have a Regulatory element. Internet alliances have a Privacy element.

When drafting each version of the Alliance Framework document, the firm's position on each element is written in prose rather than in bullet points. Ten executives listening to a bullet point presentation of a complex topic will carry away at least seven different versions of what was said. Drafting in prose ensures a com-

mon understanding among internal stakeholders and
between prospective partners. The trick to building an
effective Alliance Framework document is to ensure that
the firm's position on each element is described accurately and completely.

Alliance Framework Process

The disciplined Alliance Framework process for creating
both internal alliances and the interfirm alliance can be
viewed as a series of six steps:

> Step 1: Appointing the Planning and Negotiating
> Team
> Step 2: Achieving Internal Consensus
> Step 3: Approaching Potential Partners: Strategic
> Fit Assessment
> Step 4: Conducting Resource Fit Assessment
> Step 5: Selecting the Partner
> Step 6: Negotiating an Agreement

For clarity, we will explain these six steps as a dis-
crete series of events. However, in an actual situation the
steps overlap. Furthermore, the six-step process includes
feedback loops. For example, new information about a
potential partner revealed in steps 3, 4, or 6 will require
revisiting step 2 to ensure continued internal consensus.
In the balance of this chapter, we will describe the highlights of each step. A detailed discussion of each step will
follow in subsequent chapters.

Step 1: Appointing the Planning and Negotiating Team

We will introduce two important principles here (with more detail on team membership given in Chapter 2):

1. The Planning and Negotiating Team should be led by a line manager rather than by a staff alliance expert.
2. Every key stakeholder group must be represented on the team.

These two principles drive success. A manager with direct profit-and-loss responsibility for the business must be in charge of planning and negotiating. This ensures effective ties between the alliance and the firm's underlying business. When all stakeholder groups are represented on the Planning and Negotiating Team, internal disagreements can be exposed and resolved during the process.

Step 2: Using the Alliance Framework Document to Achieve Internal Consensus

The Planning and Negotiating Team drafts the Alliance Framework document. The leadership of every key stakeholder organization must review and approve the document. By describing elements in carefully written text, internal stakeholders understand exactly what the alliance will mean to them, including the obligations and opportunities the alliance presents.

Internal agreement is gained through an iterative review and revision process. Each key stakeholder organization reviews each version of the document.

Disagreements are exposed and resolved. Each version reflects growing internal alignment among stakeholders as the result of a systematic process of stakeholder input and dispute resolution. At the same time, each iterated version contains increasingly detailed information on such matters as the firm's positions on financial aspects and intellectual property rights. This process acts as a powerful force to create the internal alliances so important to success. If there are big internal disagreements or too many small disagreements, the time to find out is now, not six months into alliance implementation.

———

Think back to your firm's last alliance. Were internal disagreements inside the firm identified after the agreement was signed? How did you handle the disagreements? How did the partner handle them?

———

Step 3: Approaching Potential Partners: Strategic Fit Assessment

Alliance partners must fit together in two ways if they are going to succeed:

1. *Strategic fit* describes how well your firm and each prospective partner are aligned strategically.
2. *Resource fit* describes how well the resources of each prospective partner complement the resources of your firm.

Step 3 addresses strategic fit by focusing attention on a subset of Alliance Framework elements called the Strategic Assessment Elements (SAEs). These elements clearly outline each firm's strategic issues, including deal-killers. During early discussions, each side determines the strategic fit between the positions of the two firms without overexposing each other to sensitive information. The SAEs typically include Objectives, Roles, Overall Resources, Boundaries, Market Model, Intersections, and Strategic Exclusivity. If the prospective partners find that they do not share a common vision of the alliance opportunity after discussing these elements, they should part friends. There is no reason to negotiate the complexities of Intellectual Property positions and the nuances of the Financial Pie-Split if the firms do not agree on strategy.

Agreement on SAEs during step 3 does not guarantee the two firms will successfully create an alliance. Step 4 may reveal poor resource fit. Step 6 may surface disagreement on the Financial Pie-Split, Intellectual Property positions, or Term and Termination requirements. So what is the value of focusing on the SAEs in strategic fit assessment? Agreement on the SAEs greatly reduces the potential for unresolvable strategic disagreements during negotiations. Disagreement on one or more SAEs is a strong signal that the two firms are not strategically aligned. Experienced alliance companies use the level of agreement on SAEs during step 3 to make their first go/no-go decision and narrow down the list of potential partners. Disagreements that appear unresolvable during step 3 suggest that the two firms should part friends and focus their resources on more promising opportunities. Agreement means the two firms should devote the resources necessary to move through the remaining steps.

As we will discuss in Chapter 3, the Planning and Negotiating Team also uses the SAEs in the early stages of step 2 to achieve internal consensus. Stakeholder review of SAEs will quickly reveal significant internal disagreements, which must be resolved for the firm to move ahead with the alliance formation process.

Step 4: Conducting Resource Fit Assessment

The purpose of step 4 is to enable each firm to determine how well its resources fit with those of the potential partner. Assessing each firm's resources entails a series of visits to the other firm's site to assess the resources the other firm will bring to the deal. Each side is trying to answer several questions. What is the quality of the partner's resources? What is the quantity of the partner's resources? Will the combined firms provide the alliance with 100 percent of the needed resources? Too often, prospective alliance partners miss the fact that their combination yields only 90 percent of the resources needed to succeed. Each assumes that the other will bring the remaining 10 percent. Exposing resource shortfalls requires both openness and careful evaluation. The partners, after identifying shortfalls, must discuss whether additional alliance partners or contracted vendors can fill the gaps. Because of the nature of the shared information and the fact that a deal may not happen, the agendas for these visits are carefully negotiated in advance. The firms must agree on what they need to learn and what they do not have to learn. Steps 3 and 4 are governed by appropriate nondisclosure agreements (see Chapters 4 and 5).

Step 5: Selecting the Partner

The results of the assessments in steps 3 and 4 enable a company to select the best partner from an initial short list of prospective partners. During strategic fit and resource fit assessments, the identity of the optimum partner usually becomes clear to both parties. In a very real sense, the two firms select each other during steps 3 and 4. However, the deal is not yet done. Significant disagreements can still emerge in the attempt to negotiate the rest of the Alliance Framework elements.

Step 6: Negotiating an Agreement

As a final step, the prospective partners negotiate their positions on the remaining Alliance Framework elements (including Financial Pie-Split, Term and Termination, Working Process and Governance, and Intellectual Property). Additional internal versions of the Alliance Framework document are created as new issues arise, both internally among key stakeholders and externally at the negotiating table. Since the current Alliance Framework version is a complete description of the firm's positions on all aspects of the alliance, the impact of a new issue on the firm's strategy is quickly assessed.

During negotiations with the selected partner, the use of a common set of elements and an agreed-on definition for each element ensures that both firms develop the same understanding of the alliance as it takes shape, both inside their respective companies and at the negotiating table. Since the elements completely describe the key business aspects of the alliance and are negotiated in parallel, the Alliance Framework drives both firms to reveal all of their intentions *quickly*. The parallel process encourages both firms to reveal the "fun stuff" and to tackle the "not so much fun stuff" at the same time.

The deal is done when all Alliance Framework element issues are resolved at the negotiating table. The firms develop a joint Alliance Framework document incorporating the agreed positions. Legal counsels for both firms translate the joint Alliance Framework document into the final alliance contract.

How Long Does the Alliance Framework Process Take?

Speed is essential. Inefficient alliance planning and negotiations that drag on for eighteen or twenty-four months leave both firms worse off. While two firms are trying to put together an alliance, the marketplace is marching on. Competitors undistracted by lengthy alliance negotiations are aggressively engaging the marketplace. Potential alliance partners must walk away from unproductive discussions quickly and redirect resources to more attractive opportunities. The Alliance Framework process is designed to quickly get to a deal or to a friendly parting of the ways.

The timeline begins with the appointment of the Planning and Negotiating team in step 1. Top corporate management has the responsibility to make the right appointments and to ensure that team members have the time, support, and visibility required to do the job. They must also make sure that team members are held accountable for the deliverables in the Alliance Framework process. Without clear direction and follow-up by top management, the alliance planning process may degenerate into unproductive wheel-spinning.

The time required for step 2 depends on three factors. First, how carefully has the firm thought through its strategy for the business underlying the potential alliance? That is why Business Plan Summary is an Alliance Framework element; it forces all stakeholders to review the underlying business assumptions behind the prospective alliance and get disagreements ironed out. The second factor is the complexity and scope of the prospective alliance. The final factor is the role of top management in devoting the required resources to the Alliance Framework process and in resolving disagreements among stakeholders. Wise top managers insist on dedicated and disciplined Alliance Framework planning by the team and stakeholder organizations. They are sensitive to the need to step in at the right moments to resolve disagreements. In practice, we find that the time for step 2 ranges from three weeks to five weeks in firms with some Alliance Framework experience.

How much time should it take to go from approaching a potential partner (step 3) to selecting the best partner for detailed negotiations (step 5)? We use a personal target of eight to ten weeks to execute steps 3, 4, and 5. Although that may seem short, we find that when firms are serious about a prospective alliance opportunity, they devote the resources needed to carry out the required assessments. As in step 2, the time required depends on top management involvement and alliance complexity.

The time for step 6 can range from just a few weeks to several months, depending on the complexity of Alliance Framework elements beyond those addressed in step 3 and the dedication of the Planning and Negotiating Teams on both sides.

Now that we've had an overview of the Alliance Framework, the rest of the chapters in Part I will discuss the six steps and the elements in more detail.

C H A P T E R   2

APPOINTING THE PLANNING AND NEGOTIATING TEAM

Step 1 of the Alliance Framework process is appointing the Planning and Negotiating Team.

The driving force behind creating a Planning and Negotiating Team is the need to link alliance formation and business strategy. As discussed in Chapter 1, effective alliance planning begins after a business strategy is in place and understood within the firm. When that strategy includes the possibility of one or more alliances, the firm appoints a team to begin alliance planning. In some situations, that planning begins by assessing whether an alliance is the best way to achieve the strategic goals or whether another method (including "going it alone") might be better. In other cases, the need for one or more alliances is clear, and the Planning and Negotiating Team begins the Alliance Framework process.

But why appoint a team? Why not ask an experienced alliance person and a lawyer to plan the prospective deal, pick the partner, and negotiate the terms of the agreement? The reasons should be clear after reading Chapter 1. Alliance success is dependent on achieving connections among the terms of the alliance, the business intent, and the commitment of internal stakeholder groups. That can only be done by engaging a team of people who represent all relevant stakeholders.

Now let's look at team membership. The underlying idea is to bring together the people needed to transform strategic intent into the terms of an alliance agreement. Those terms must be agreeable to internal stakeholders as well as the external partner. Remember the "three alliances in one" phenomenon? Experienced executives manage all three alliances simultaneously by forming a team made up of members with the following characteristics:

1. A clearly identified Team Leader
2. Representatives of stakeholder groups who must provide resources to the alliance during implementation
3. People who will play leading day-to-day implementation roles
4. People who bring specialized skills to the alliance planning and negotiating process

How those characteristics are best used to determine the membership of a particular Planning and Negotiating Team depends on the nature of the alliance, the organization structure, the management style of the firm, and the skills of specific individuals.

MicroCATS at Battelle: The Oil Industry Alliance

We will use Battelle Memorial Institute's commercialization strategy for one of its innovative technologies as an excellent example of how a clearly understood strategy leads to the establishment of an appropriate team. In Chapters 3 and 4, we will follow Battelle's team through internal planning and approaches to potential alliance partners.

Genesis of the MicroCATS Alliance

Wayne Simmons is an engineer and business executive who creates value by integrating powerful business models with powerful technologies. By combining a novel technology with an alliance among competitors, he will help the oil industry carry out many of its operations at smaller scales than previously possible, permitting cost-effective and environmentally favorable processing in remote or decentralized locations. Here's his story.

It all started with his Ph.D. in engineering and a deep desire to make a difference. While working at Battelle Memorial Institute,* Wayne was responsible for the commercial development of MicroCATS technology. MicroCATS involves the use of narrow channel catalytic reactors to improve the efficiency and lower the cost of chemical processing. The technology works by increasing both the speed of movement of chemicals that must be

---

* Battelle Memorial Institute is a not-for-profit technical firm that develops new technologies and products for industry and government. Its industrial work ranges from medical products and pharmaceuticals to innovations for the automotive, chemical, and agrochemical industries. It develops solutions for government in areas such as the environment, national security, transportation, and health and human services. Battelle has a staff of 7,500 scientists, engineers, and support specialists.

brought together for a chemical reaction, and the rate at which heat is transferred into or out of the processing equipment. In addition, MicroCATS technology lowers the cost of the processing equipment, especially when relatively small quantities of chemicals are used. MicroCATS is part of a larger Battelle effort on microtechnology at the Department of Energy's Pacific Northwest National Laboratory and at Battelle's Columbus, Ohio facility.

Wayne and Battelle's development staff realized that MicroCATS technology could have many uses in the oil industry, in applications such as natural gas processing, crude oil refining, and petrochemical manufacturing. By using MicroCATS to reduce the size and cost of processing equipment, oil companies can carry out important operations in remote locations where relatively small quantities of oil and gas are available to be processed into usable products. With conventional processing equipment, some materials are not being utilized since the costs of processing or transportation is too high.

Wayne's team was convinced that MicroCATS technology could greatly reduce the size and cost of processing equipment for many chemical processes. Battelle's scale-up calculations showed that MicroCATS could make these processes economically viable in remote oil fields or petrochemical plants. However, like many technologies that work in the laboratory, there were still open questions. Would this gizmo operate reliably in remote and inhospitable locations, on a very large scale, in an oil field or petrochemical plant producing at full blast? And would the economic projections work out in practice? It would take substantial funds and a test site to answer those questions. Battelle had been Wayne's venture capitalist, but it could not bankroll the project much longer. Wayne needed real money and he needed it fast.

The first thought was to approach traditional venture capitalists, but there are downsides to venture capital financing. Wayne and the development group realized that the best people to fund the project were the oil companies with the problems. Besides money, oil companies could provide access to test sites, knowledge of oil engineering and petrochemical practices, and insights into how the oil industry makes the decisions to deploy new technologies. In the end, it was the oil companies that would make the capital investment decisions to deploy MicroCATS technology in the field. Battelle had to get them involved early.

Wayne had to consider another knotty problem of oil company funding and involvement. The first application at remote oil company facilities was just the tip of the iceberg. MicroCATS technology has many applications in the chemical industry. If this first project proved that MicroCATS was economical on a large scale, it could be commercialized in a variety of areas. Battelle's oil company partners for the initial application might not be the best partners for other applications. How could Battelle maintain its ability to independently exploit MicroCATS in other areas even though the oil companies were funding the first commercial application? How could Battelle politely un-invite them to the follow-up parties, while using the intellectual property created during the first oil industry application and compensating the oil companies for their contributions?

Using the Alliance Framework to Establish Team Roles

Good timing plays a part in every story like this. While

Battelle's R&D staff was developing MicroCATS technology, Battelle top management adopted the Alliance Framework as the standard alliance creation process for the firm. To ensure that alliance creation and management became a core competence of the firm, top management, business unit heads, and every business development manager went through Alliance Framework training. This juxtaposition of need and resources provided Wayne with access to alliance experts and a supportive organization. Wayne realized that the Alliance Framework would enable him to build strong internal alliances as well as the external alliance. In planning the MicroCATS alliance, Wayne needed to achieve alignment among several Battelle groups that were thousands of miles apart and widely separated in the Battelle organizational chart. Wayne hoped that the oil company partners would use the Alliance Framework to achieve their own internal alignment.

Wayne thought about path dependence and the need to clearly understand long-term strategy. He realized that moving MicroCATS technology from the laboratory to its first full-scale industrial application required the planning and negotiation of a complex development and commercialization alliance. The Alliance Framework would have to solve the problems Wayne anticipated, as well as problems he had not yet thought about. The alliance must be acceptable to the Battelle development community, to Battelle's top management, and the management of the oil company partners. He began by assembling the Planning and Negotiating Team to deal with these issues.

Team Leader

The identity of the Team Leader depends on the nature

and scope of the alliance and on the management structure of the firm. The Team Leader should be a senior manager of the organization at the "business center" of the alliance. He or she must be viewed as someone who can speak internally for the business center organization and externally for the entire firm. The Team Leader is the person top corporate management expects to hold responsible for implementation success after the alliance is created. This means that a line manager, not a lawyer or a business development manager, should lead the Planning and Negotiating Team.

What is the business center of an alliance? Generally, it is the internal organization whose success is most closely connected to the success of the alliance. For firms organized into strategic business units (SBU), each with its own profit/loss and functional responsibilities, the Team Leader for a product development and marketing alliance might be the SBU head or one of his direct reports. The Team Leader for an R&D alliance might be the laboratory director or other R&D manager responsible for the relevant technology area.

The identification of the business center is less clear in situations where the prospective alliance cuts across multiple SBUs. It is also less clear when a firm with a centralized functional structure is planning an alliance cutting across multiple functions. In those cases, the Team Leader is selected from one of the key stakeholder organizations, based on the person's ability to lead the process. That process leadership role involves using the Alliance Framework to expose disagreements among stakeholder groups, getting disagreements resolved, and ensuring that stakeholders commit the required resources.

Why should the Team Leader be a senior person? The Alliance Framework process forces the organization to link business strategy, alliance planning, negotiations, and implementation. Those linkages require decisions, resources, and time commitments from key people. Only a senior line manager at the business center of the alliance has the power or influence to shift resources from internal projects and focus people's energies on the alliance.

When we make this point to top corporate executives, we often encounter two objections. One is that the person with profit-and-loss responsibility is too busy to lead a Planning and Negotiating Team. The other is that the person is inexperienced in alliances and does not have the background to deal with the planning and negotiation issues that lie ahead.

We believe that the "busy" objection requires top management to review whether the prospective alliance is important enough to move forward. The time and energy of the Team Leader is only a small portion of the resources needed to successfully form and implement the alliance. The line manager as Team Leader will delegate much of the time-consuming work to other team members. The "inexperience" objection is also not valid. Alliance planning and negotiation is a learnable skill, and the Team Leader will rely on the expertise of team members with alliance experience to deal with the sticky problems during planning and negotiation.

Ben Maiden, Wayne's boss, asked Wayne to personally lead the Planning and Negotiating Team. As the executive responsible for the development and commercialization of MicroCATS technology, Wayne was well positioned to deal with internal disagreements between business strategy and alliance planning. He was also the logical person to lead Battelle in partner selection and negotiations. Ben and Wayne knew that other firms use business development managers or lawyers to lead teams, but those managers cannot drive strategic decisions or shift resources to planning and negotiating tasks. Wayne could and would do that.

Although not a day-by-day team member, Ben Maiden played a crucial internal role as the Planning and Negotiating Team began its planning efforts. As a top corporate executive, Ben was able to help Wayne and his team maintain the support of Battelle's top management. For example, Wayne's project competed with other promising Battelle programs for scarce financial and human resources. Wayne had to report regularly to the Investment Committee, Battelle's senior management group responsible for allocating resources to promising new initiatives. As a member of the Investment Committee, Ben informally briefed other members on the team's status and provided timely feedback to Wayne on top management concerns. As Ben became convinced of the project's promise, he became an important project supporter at the highest level of Battelle.

─────

In your firm, where should Planning and Negotiating Team Leaders be found in the organizational structure?

─────

Stakeholder Representatives

Team members representing key stakeholder groups perform two distinct functions during the planning and negotiating process. First, they bring specific functional expertise. For example, in an alliance involving the manufacture of a jointly developed product, a team member from the manufacturing organization is responsible for developing the firm's positions on prospective manufacturing capital investment and unit costs. Equally important, that person acts as the ambassador between the manufacturing group and the Planning and Negotiating Team. By sharing manufacturing's viewpoint with the team and keeping manufacturing's management informed of the latest team thinking, the ambassador prevents misunderstandings and surprises. Any differences between the manufacturing group's and the team's positions must be exposed and resolved. While the ambassador is the informal communication channel, each version of the Alliance Framework document is the formal channel for communicating the commitments that the manufacturing group is expected to make.

Most of MicroCATS R&D was done at the Department of Energy's Pacific Northwest National Laboratory (PNNL) in Richland, Washington. That federal laboratory is managed by Battelle. In addition to the first oil industry applications, PNNL staff members were working on a number of other MicroCATS projects. They had a deep interest in how the first project would be brought to market, with strong opinions on what should be done by Battelle's Columbus commercialization group. Much of the ongoing Battelle work in the alliance would be carried out by scientists and engineers at PNNL. Therefore, it was essential that the Planning and Negotiating Team include a strong stakeholder representative from PNNL.

Fortunately, such a person was in place. Laura Silva had been a key contributor in creating the initial commercialization strategy for MicroCATS. She had a strong technical and business background, with high credibility at PNNL. Besides being the PNNL stakeholder representative, Laura became Wayne's deputy on the team. She also played a vital role in approaching potential partners and assessing their strategic and resource fits, as we will see in Chapter 4.

Byron Sohovich from Battelle's financial group brought specialized financial skills to the Planning and Negotiating Team and represented an important stakeholder. Battelle's intent was to use alliances to expand its business. Battelle's financial community, up through Mark Kontos, the CFO, was dedicated to that business expansion. They had an important stake in the success of Wayne's project. Part of Byron's team responsibilities was to keep the financial community well connected to the team's work.

Battelle had established a strategic planning group to work on business plans for new initiatives and to ensure that each initiative was consistent with corporate strategy. To keep the project closely tied to Battelle's strategy, Mike Eggett of the strategic planning group was appointed to the team. Mike not only kept the connection to strategy alive and well, but he also worked on the ties between MicroCATS business planning and the Alliance Framework elements.

Implementation Leaders and Continuity

When implementation begins, all of the efforts invested in planning and negotiation must be transformed into day-to-day working relationships. These working relationships must be established between the parties and among stakeholder groups inside each firm. Chapter 9 describes management tools to help establish those relationships once implementation begins. But beyond these tools, alliance implementation gets off to a fast start when both partners assign key implementers to the Planning and Negotiating Teams. Through their early participation, these people translate contractual language into everyday reality. By being part of the alliance formation process, they understand the explicit and implicit expectations of both sides. Team participation also allows the implementers on both sides to build the interpersonal relationships that are important to success.

Teams can have one or more people who will play a significant implementation role. Depending on the specific situation, there are several options. One approach is to identify a single team member as the prospective alliance Operating Manager who will be responsible for the ongoing relationship between the partners during implementation. Being an alliance Operating Manager is often a full-time job. That person must coordinate the internal resources of the firm and integrate them with those of the partner. That job must be done with a clear understanding of the terms of the deal and the expectations on both sides for alliance deliverables. Sometimes, for very significant alliances involving major business unit resources on both sides, the Team Leader might also be the designated alliance Operating Manager. For alliances of more limited scope, a less senior person on the team can be designated.

Another approach is to identify several Planning and Negotiating Team members who will play important roles in implementation, with specific responsibilities to be determined later. That's what happened in the Battelle MicroCATS alliance. Wayne, Laura, and other team members all took on significant implementation assignments.

Specialized Skills: Business Development Manager

The Business Development Manager is the person who brings alliance expertise to the Planning and Negotiating Team. This person will guide the team through the Alliance Framework process. The Business Development Manager will do much of the detailed internal work, such as planning and facilitating internal team meetings, writing each iterated version of the Alliance Framework document, following up on task assignments of team members, and proposing solutions to stakeholder disagreements on Alliance Framework elements. The Business Development Manager usually participates in negotiations with prospective partners.

Some firms appoint people working in business development to lead the alliance formation process. We believe that is a mistake. By placing the business development function at the center of the process, rather than as a supporting skill, the firm creates an immediate gap between business intent and the alliance. Because the Alliance Framework was new to Battelle, Wayne asked Battelle's external consultants to carry out the Business Development Manager role on the Planning and Negotiating Team.

Legal Support

Alliance formation and structure are strongly influenced by the law. Every Planning and Negotiating Team should have one or more lawyers as members. Some executives are reluctant to include lawyers on the team for several reasons. A common view is that lawyers add little to the early stages of the alliance planning and negotiation process, and they create barriers to progress if brought in too early. Those perceived barriers arise from a view that legal people will "tell us what we can't do." Executives also worry that the presence of lawyers will chill the atmosphere during early stages of talks between prospective partners.

These attitudes lead companies to underutilize lawyers during the planning and negotiation process. The value added by lawyers depends on the skills, experience, and temperament of the individual lawyer. Executives who complain about limited value and barrier creation have the wrong lawyer. The right lawyer will add both legal and business insights to the Alliance Framework process, often serving as a useful counterpoint to other team members. Experienced legal counsel will also identify legal issues that are not apparent to other Planning and Negotiating Team members.

There is another way that the right lawyer contributes to the success of the Alliance Framework process. A lawyer who is deeply involved in the internal planning and external negotiation process develops an accurate understanding of the business intent of managers on both sides. That understanding is a critical element in accurately translating those business intents into contract language. The impact of this translation pitfall can be underestimated. We are often called in to diagnose and treat sick alliances. As a first step, we read the alliance contract. A common source of difficulty is a contract that does not properly reflect the intents of the business people who planned the deal. That type of alliance distress is a direct result of contracts being drafted by lawyers who were not closely connected to the business discussions.

The assignment of lawyers to Planning and

Negotiating Teams depends on the complexity of the alliance and how the firm's legal support is organized. Sometimes a single attorney, either in-house or outside counsel, should be on the team. That lawyer contributes to the entire planning and negotiating process, consulting offline with other specialized lawyers on an as-needed basis. Alternatively, more than one lawyer can be appointed to the team and participate regularly in the team's work. That is how Battelle organized legal participation for the first MicroCATS project. Bob Zeig, the head of Battelle's intellectual property law group, Tom Sharpe, an experienced contract attorney, and Dan O'Brien, a tax and financial law specialist, were all involved.

Who are the most likely members of a Planning and Negotiating Team inside your firm?

Tips for Completing Step 1 of the Alliance Framework

When you create your Planning and Negotiating Team, remember to:

- Create a clear channel between the team and top corporate management.
- Emphasize the importance of linking alliance planning to business strategy.
- Ensure that the Team Leader is a senior person at the business center of the alliance.

WHAT IF THE PROSPECTIVE PARTNER WANTS TO USE A DIFFERENT TEAM?

Perhaps the partner wants to use a Planning and Negotiating Team membership different from yours. While we advocate the team structure described in this chapter, as shown in Battelle's approach, not every firm agrees with us. Some firms use alliance negotiation teams led by business development specialists supported by lawyers and other staff. Line managers and other internal stakeholders are not team members, and business development managers are expected to keep line organizations appraised of alliance planning and negotiations. We believe that such a team structure creates a risk of internal conflicts since important stakeholders are not tied tightly to alliance formation. Should you always walk away from such a partner, based on your concern over internal conflicts on their side of the deal? Generally, no. But this situation is a warning flag of possible trouble. During the negotiations, your firm must find ways to confirm that the partner firm's stakeholders have bought into the deal, to avoid unpleasant surprises after implementation begins. In practice, that's hard to do. For example, some insights into the attitudes of the partner's stakeholders can be achieved during the Tirekicks described in Chapter 5. But there is no real substitute for ongoing close involvement of stakeholders on both sides of the entire planning and negotiating process, which is why we advocate that as part of the Alliance Framework.

- Get representation from all key stakeholders who must budget resources for the alliance during the first twenty-four months of the relationship.
- Include legal representation on the Planning and Negotiating Team and any other staff function that is needed (e.g., finance and tax).
- Ensure the likely alliance Operating Manager is a member of the team.
- Plan for continuity of some team members into implementation.
- Get appropriate alliance specialists on the team.

CHAPTER 3

USING THE ALLIANCE FRAMEWORK PROCESS AND DOCUMENT TO ACHIEVE INTERNAL CONSENSUS

Now that the Planning and Negotiating Team is in place, the work of achieving internal consensus begins. The goal is to ensure that every key stakeholder understands the firm's positions on the alliance and agrees to support them. To do that, the team creates draft positions on each Alliance Framework element, generates an Alliance Framework document, and sends that document to every stakeholder for input. Those inputs are used to refine the document and generate the next version. The process continues until all key stakeholders understand the goals and objectives of the alliance and agree to commit their resources during implementation.

"Consensus" does not mean that a few stakeholders have a vague understanding and general feeling of support for a possible alliance. That kind of weak support leads to disaster when stakeholders realize they are involved in a poorly understood relationship. Things go from bad to worse when stakeholders realize that their resources have been committed without their full knowledge and support. The consensus achieved in step 2 is sharply focused. The Alliance Framework document, and discussions based on that document, ensure that all stakeholders are informed about all aspects of the prospective alliance and what that alliance means to their jobs. Most important, all stakeholders are expected to comment, add value based on their own expertise and responsibilities, and speak frankly about any objections. The Planning and Negotiating Team builds these stakeholder inputs into iterated versions of the Alliance Framework document. The process allows the firm to identify, debate, and resolve conflicting stakeholder views through the firm's management decision-making process.

The Planning and Negotiating Team is at the center of step 2 of the Alliance Framework. It creates each iterated version of the document, discusses issues with stakeholders, and drives management decisions to resolve disagreements. "Consensus" doesn't necessarily mean that every stakeholder is happy as alliance planning goes forward. But it does mean that all stakeholders have the opportunity to air their views and understand the organizational commitments that the prospective alliance will require. After the stakeholder inputs in step 2, the firm's management makes an informed decision whether to proceed to step 3 and beyond. Let's follow Battelle as the team creates internal consensus for the MicroCATS project introduced in Chapter 2.

Teaching the Team About the Alliance Framework

Having been through Battelle's Alliance Framework training program, Wayne Simmons led the first meeting. Since he knew that some team members were new to alliances and that most had not received Alliance Framework training, the meeting began with an interactive tutorial on the Alliance Framework tool. The Planning and Negotiating Team learned about the links between strategy and alliances, and about the impacts of path dependence discussed in Chapter 1. They discussed common pitfalls in alliance planning and negotiations, such as the lack of internal and external strategic alignment, negotiations that discuss the "fun stuff" but delay discussion of deal-killers, and the problems of exposure to proprietary information of prospective partners. The tutorial went on to explain the Alliance Framework process and document, typical definitions of Alliance Framework elements, and how the process and document should be adapted to Battelle's organizational structure and management style.

SAEs Help in Achieving Internal Consensus

During the Alliance Framework tutorial, the Battelle team discussed the role of the Strategic Assessment Elements (SAEs). The SAEs are a subset of the Alliance Framework elements that focus on key strategic elements of the alliance. They are used to achieve internal consensus in step 2 and to assess the strategic fit of each prospective partner in step 3.

Wayne pointed out that there is an important reason for concentrating on the SAEs during the initial stages of step 2. The Planning and Negotiating Team can generate draft positions on SAEs quickly, and early versions of the Alliance Framework document, focused on the SAEs, can be circulated to stakeholders for comment. That enables stakeholders to provide timely strategic input to the team while detailed work on elements other than the SAEs goes on in parallel. If strong internal disagreements by key stakeholders on one or more SAEs prove to be unresolvable, that might lead the firm's management to redirect the team's planning activities away from the prospective alliance toward other options for achieving the firm's strategic intent. With the focused internal reviews built into the Alliance Framework process, that no-go situation should emerge quickly in step 2.

Selecting the SAEs for the MicroCATS Oil Industry Alliance

As the team began to discuss the SAEs for the MicroCATS oil industry alliance, it seemed that people were talking past one another. During the initial discussion, each Planning and Negotiating Team member spoke about an issue that concerned him or her, such as how tasks should be divided between Battelle and an oil company or what knowledge an oil company had to bring to the alliance. Wayne pointed out that the first order of business was to develop a list of SAEs that were relevant to this alliance. But how could that be done in a systematic way?

The team used the typical list of SAEs in Figure 3-1 as the basis for a brainstorming discussion. The purpose of the discussion was to identify key issues that impact on one or more SAEs. Beginning with the Objectives element, the Planning and Negotiating Team captured issues such as:

- What oil industry challenge should Battelle select as the first application for this technology?
- What do Battelle and its oil company partner intend to achieve, anticipating that their intentions may be somewhat different?
- What functions will Battelle carry out, and what will the oil company do?
- What technical capabilities and other assets will both bring to the alliance?
- What products or services will be included in the alliance, understanding that MicroCATS technology has many other applications?
- To what extent may Battelle and the oil company form similar relationships with others, given that this alliance may involve more than one oil company?
- What will other marketplace participants see as they look into the alliance, since Battelle and an oil company partner are in very different businesses?
- What contractual or business constraints do either

Battelle or the oil company have that would impact on this alliance?

● How could profits from the initial installations and subsequent applications be allocated between Battelle and a partner?

● How could Battelle ensure that it had the necessary rights to exploit new developments coming out of the alliance?

Figure 3-1. The Strategic Assessment Elements.

● Objectives
  ○ Ours
  ○ Theirs

● Roles
  ○ Ours
  ○ Theirs

● Overall Resources
  ○ Ours
  ○ Theirs

● Boundaries

● Market Model

● Strategic Exclusivity

● Intersection

Developing Battelle's Positions on the SAEs

Starting with the list of SAEs and key issues, the Planning and Negotiating Team worked on developing Battelle's positions. They prepared alternative positions on some SAEs, knowing that a potential alliance partner might have contrasting but acceptable views. Wayne directed the discussion, with the alliance consultant writing substantive points on flipcharts taped to the walls. When there was significant disagreement, or not enough information to develop a final position, that was also written on the flipcharts. Because a complete vision of the alliance for the step 2 internal review, and later for the step 3 strategic fit assessment, required addressing all SAEs in parallel, Wayne pushed the team to avoid getting bogged down in debate on one or two elements. The team moved quickly through the entire SAE list by concentrating on major issues in each element.

Our Objectives and Their Objectives

Objectives should be specific and tightly tied to the company's strategy. The team's first thoughts for Our Objectives were very broad: "Become the leading firm in the field," and "Create a profitable business for Battelle." But the team realized that these statements are just as relevant to the local gas station as they are to Battelle. A new metric was born, which was dubbed the "gas station test." Any Objectives statement that was as applicable to the local gas station as it was to Battelle was scratched off the flipchart list.

The Planning and Negotiating Team then started to

develop Objectives that were aimed specifically at this alliance: "Create cost-effective processing in remote oil company locations." "Prove the commercial feasibility of MicroCATS technology." "Open up the potential for subsequent MicroCATS applications." While such high-level statements are useful and should be included as Our Objectives, they are inadequate. Our Objectives is the foundation for the firm's positions on all other Alliance Framework elements. It must contain specific statements of intent that tie to those other elements. Most important, there must be no conflicts between an Our Objectives statement and any position in another Alliance Framework element. If a conflict appears during internal planning or during negotiations, either the statement of Our Objectives or the firm's position in the other Alliance Framework element must be modified to remove the conflict.

An example from Battelle's oil company alliance will illustrate the problem. A Battelle strategic intent was to maintain control of the MicroCATS technology for purposes beyond the first commercial application. Battelle might not want to involve oil company partners in those other applications. Therefore, the Planning and Negotiating Team drafted the following Our Objectives statement:

Battelle wishes to maintain control of MicroCATS applications beyond the initial application, and have no obligation (other than as agreed in the Financial Pie-Split element) to involve its oil company partner in those other applications.

This statement on MicroCATS control had to be consistent with other Alliance Framework elements. For example, the Roles element would specify that Battelle would control third-party involvement in all other applications. The Intellectual Property element (to be negotiated in step 6) would provide rights for Battelle to exploit new developments coming out of the alliance, independently of the oil company partner. This means that the oil company partner would have to forgo rights to those new developments. The reference to the Financial Pie-Split element was an acknowledgment that an oil company partner might expect a share of the financial return from Battelle's independent exploitation of cooperative developments.

Why do we emphasize the need for consistency between Our Objectives statements and all other Alliance Framework elements? Because that consistency is vital to achieve two important goals during alliance planning and negotiation:

1. Keep the alliance terms aligned with strategy.
2. Keep all internal stakeholders together as the alliance takes shape.

Without a systematic way of keeping the ties between strategy and alliance terms visible to all stakeholders, it is easy for an alliance to deviate from the initially conceived strategy during the negotiation process. The consistency requirement forces the firm, at all levels, to face up to conflicts as they arise and to deal thoughtfully with possible impacts on strategy. We do not suggest that every aspect of initial strategy is cast in concrete at the start of the Alliance Framework process. In this example, Battelle might revisit its initial strategy and agree to involve an oil company in one or more future applications. That would result in a modification to the Our Objectives element.

But the consistency requirement forces the firm to deliberately expose the strategic modification to all stakeholders. That avoids the "I never knew that was part of the deal" problem, which can torpedo alliances during implementation.

The Planning and Negotiating Team went on to add many more specific Our Objectives statements. Two examples were:

> Deploy the first full-scale MicroCATS application at an oil company partner site by 20xx.
>
> Acquire $xxx from oil company partners to cover part of cash needs until positive cash flow begins in 20yy.

The team spent a few minutes preparing statements of Their Objectives. How could Battelle's Team know the objectives of a potential oil company partner? The Team made educated guesses, based on earlier informal discussions with six oil companies on the MicroCATS opportunity. The purpose of those guesses was to anticipate oil company needs and formulate appropriate Battelle positions.

Our Roles, Their Roles

The Roles elements contain careful statements of "who does what" in the alliance, including typical functions such as product specifications, product portfolio selection, equipment design, manufacturing, and sales. For the MicroCATS alliance, the Planning and Negotiating Team prepared a detailed list of scientific and engineering tasks. Going beyond broad categories like equipment design, the team considered such tasks as design and production of the full-scale versions of the laboratory-size devices built at Battelle. Projecting Battelle and oil company capabilities to carry out each task, the team made prospective assignments for each. For certain tasks, the team specified that responsibilities would be shared. The team knew that task assignments might be modified based on step 3 (strategic fit assessment) and on specific capabilities of each prospective oil company partner as revealed in step 4 (resource fit assessment). The initial task list would be the starting point for Roles discussions in step 3 and beyond.

———

In your firm's alliance planning process, how carefully do you plan and document Objectives as an early step? How are those Objectives linked to strategy?

———

For each task, the team also specified decision-making guidelines. In a healthy alliance, both partners exchange ideas on all tasks. But there is a fundamental issue. Will the alliance use a "one partner" or "consensual" decision-making structure? In the "one partner" structure, one partner has the authority to make each major decision in its area of expertise. In a consensual structure, both firms must agree on each decision. During the Alliance Framework tutorial, the team learned that a disadvantage of "consensual" alliances, as compared with "one partner" alliances, is that consensus-building can slow things down; but the need for interpartner agreement also creates a healthy working environment and lowers the risk of alienating the partners during implementation. While there is no generally applicable right answer, the Planning and Negotiating Team considered each task separately from the point of view of the tradeoff involved and formulated Battelle's positions.

The Use of Third Parties. When a partner is assigned a Role, it does not always mean that the firm must carry out that task itself. It could mean that the partner is responsible for having the task carried out by a third party. In alliance parlance, this is referred to as a "have done" right. For example, the Planning and Negotiating Team was confident in Battelle's ability to carry out most research activities for the oil industry alliance. But it also knew that Battelle might not have all the required scientific resources to carry out some specialized tasks. The Our Roles element specified where Battelle could implement a "have done" right to hire outside experts while still maintaining responsibility for completing the work on time.

The team also considered to what extent the oil company partner could use external technical skills to execute their tasks as the MicroCATS laboratory work was scaled up. The team's best judgments were captured in the Their Roles element, with the understanding that potential partners would react to those positions in step 3.

Our Overall Resources, Their Overall Resources

The Overall Resources element describes "who brings what" to the alliance. It covers items such as intellectual property, manufacturing and sales resources, specific R&D competence, and funding. The word *overall* means that the resources are not quantified. For example, the team could not yet quantify engineering budgets for the scale-up work for the first application. Such specifics would be developed in the Detailed Resources element, in cooperation with the selected partner in step 6.

The Planning and Negotiating Team found that many of the Overall Resources statements were straightforward. Battelle would bring existing intellectual property and skills in MicroCATS technology, and an oil company would provide knowledge of production technology and access to existing installations for the first full-scale implementation. But the sources of some resources were less obvious to the team and were left open for step 3 discussions. For example, it was not clear whether an oil company could provide all the funding required, and it was possible that certain engineering expertise was outside the capability of either Battelle or an oil company. Looking ahead to step 3, the team made a careful effort to list all the resources that would be required for alliance success, including those where the source was uncertain.

Boundaries

The purpose of the Boundaries element is to clearly state the scope of the alliance. Inside the Boundaries, the firms are allied and will agree to a specific set of rules. Outside the Boundaries, the firms are not allied and will follow a different set of rules. The challenge is to make sure that both alliance partners understand the Boundaries and agree on them.

Poorly defined Boundaries build conflict into alliances. Figure 3-2 illustrates why. Let's assume that Company A and Company B have agreed to use each other's preexisting intellectual property, including certain trade secrets, inside the Boundaries of an alliance. If

Company A thinks the Boundaries look like the left circle in Figure 3-2, and Company B thinks the Boundaries look like the right circle, the alliance starts out in trouble. As long as Company B uses Company A's trade secrets in the shaded area, both sides are happy. But as soon as Company B starts using Company A's trade secrets outside the shaded area (say, at point 1), Company A feels betrayed.

Figure 3-2. Boundaries conflict.

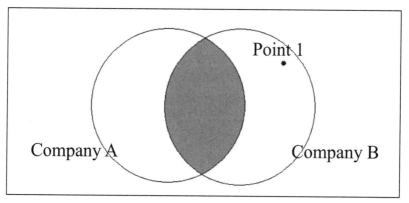

Define the Boundaries of your most prominent alliance. Would your partner agree with your definition?

It is easy to see how this problem can arise. Point 1 is a product that Company B believes is inside the Boundaries. In the minds of Company B's management, it is perfectly legitimate to use Company A's trade secrets in that product. From Company A's perspective, point 1 is outside the agreed area of cooperation. In fact, if

Company A's strategic intent is to develop that product with another partner, Company A is now constrained.

While Boundaries violations can be deliberate, they often stem from a lack of clarity during the alliance formation process. A Boundaries misunderstanding has the unfortunate by-product of creating mistrust that carries over into other areas of the relationship. In the example from Figure 3-2, we can expect that Company A's anger will poison the working relationships in the shaded area.

Defining Boundaries is an art, not a science. In our experience, the most effective method is to define the Boundaries along the following dimensions:

- Technology
- Products/Processes
- Applications/Markets
- Geography

Take the case of an exclusive deal between a large pharmaceutical company and a small inhalation-therapy firm specializing in diabetes. If the Boundaries are defined too narrowly, the small inhalation-therapy firm may be able to work with a competitor of the large pharmaceutical company on a project that the larger firm believes should fall inside the exclusive relationship. If Boundaries are defined too broadly, the small inhalation-therapy firm may be tied to the large pharmaceutical company in unintended ways. The solution is to define the Boundaries along the four dimensions and combine the dimensions using Boolean logic (i.e., and/or/not statements). For example, if the large pharmaceutical company wanted to sell the inhalation firm's product in the North American market, the Boundaries might look like this:

Technology = Inhalation therapy
and
Applications = Diabetes treatment, not injectable
and
Product = Inhalation firm's product
and
Geography = North America, not rest of world

The sum total of the statements clearly defines the Boundaries. Most alliance Boundary statements can be constructed by linking the technology, products/processes, applications/markets, and geography descriptors with Boolean logic statements. Sometimes additional descriptors are needed for specialized alliances.

Consider your firm's most prominent alliance. Have the Boundaries changed over time? Was that change agreed upon, or did the alliance evolve over time as a result of changing business conditions?

Trigger Points. Boundaries can be tied to "trigger points." A trigger point is an event specified in the Boundaries element that will modify the Boundaries in a specific way. For example, my firm and your firm may agree that you will market my firm's Products A and B. We could further agree that once sales of Products A and B reach a combined annual total of $50 million, your firm will also market my Product C. We have agreed to expand the Boundaries to include Product C after an annual sales trigger point is met.

The trigger point negotiation provides insight into strategic intent. My firm may be unwilling to entrust marketing of Product C to your firm until you have demonstrated the ability to successfully market the first two products. By agreeing to a trigger point, my firm is signaling that we intend to use your company to market Product C if you are successful with the Products A and B. In fact, the presence of the trigger point in our alliance agreement constrains my firm, since we have an obligation to grant you marketing rights to Product C under specifically defined circumstances. But suppose that my firm would not agree to a trigger point for Product C, and instead insists that Product C remain outside the Boundaries. That signals something quite different. Whatever my firm's plans are for Product C, they do not involve your firm. Trigger points in the Boundaries element send a strategic signal and are a good example of how SAEs are applied in step 3 to assess strategic fit.

The Planning and Negotiating Team at Battelle expected to ask an oil company partner to work exclusively with Battelle on MicroCATS technology for the first application, and to cooperate in that opportunity worldwide. But Battelle's strategy for MicroCATS made it critical for the applications dimension to be carefully stated in the Boundaries element. The Battelle team's intent was to form an alliance for that initial application only, without assuming that the selected oil company partners would participate in development of other commercial applications of MicroCATS. The applications dimension was written to make this clear. The products dimension was unnecessary for this alliance, since the application dimension was an adequate descriptor.

The team's first thought was to define the technology dimension as "MicroCATS technology." However, that definition was inadequate and could lead to serious misunderstandings. To protect Battelle's interests and to keep an oil company partner focused on the alliance, the team realized that the technology dimension had to be carefully written. It had to include innovations beyond MicroCATS technology as that technology existed at the start of the alliance. However, the team anticipated that any prospective partner might expect to be free to work on other innovative production approaches, independently of Battelle. How should the technology dimension be defined to simultaneously deal with both needs? A narrow dimension might allow an oil company to pursue a minor variation of MicroCATS without Battelle. But a broad dimension might require the oil company to prematurely commit to Battelle's approach.

The Planning and Negotiating Team developed a technology definition that seemed to meet both needs, extending beyond the existing MicroCATS technology but stopping well short of all potential production approaches. The team knew that the technology definition for the Boundaries element would be a key issue in step 3.

Market Model

The Market Model element addresses one fundamental question: What does the alliance look like from the customer's vantage point? Depending on the nature of the alliance, that basic question breaks down into other, more specific questions, such as:

- Who will be seen as the marketing and sales partner?

- Will the product or service be sold, leased, or licensed?
- Whose brand will be on the product or service?
- How will the partners be identified on labels and other types of marketing communications?
- Who will the customer look to for technical and logistical support?
- How will billing, warranties, and other commercial functions be handled?

The purpose of the Market Model element is to ensure that the alliance planners and negotiators look at the alliance from the customer perspective. For the oil industry alliance, the Battelle Planning and Negotiating Team considered how the developed technology would be marketed to the rest of the industry. The team identified a host of tough questions: Would the technology be licensed to users, allowing them to acquire the necessary equipment and carry out the process at their own installations? Would equipment suppliers be licensed to supply MicroCATs equipment to the rest of the oil industry? Would Battelle or the oil company partner provide some production system components to users? Would other oil companies welcome marketing efforts driven by Battelle's partner, a competitor of those later users? Would those potential customers view Battelle, an R&D company outside the industry, as a credible source of proven technology? Could Battelle market the technology and handle the many customer support functions?

Based on their knowledge of the industry and the preliminary discussions with oil companies, the team created initial Battelle positions for the Market Model element. They knew that these positions might be modified after step 3 discussions began with prospective partners.

Strategic Exclusivity

The Strategic Exclusivity element describes the extent to which either partner can enter into a similar or overlapping relationship with third parties inside the Boundaries. This element is tied to the Roles and Resources elements and must be consistent with other elements such as Intellectual Property and the Market Model.

Strategic Exclusivity can be dependent on parameters such as geography, field of use, and time. For example, Company A can have an exclusive right to jointly market Company B's product in North America, and a nonexclusive marketing right elsewhere. Or Company A's exclusive rights in North America can have a time limit during which Company A gets a head start in return for its efforts in developing that regional market.

There is a trap in the Strategic Exclusivity element where the relationship between partners is partly or completely exclusive. In an exclusive technology/marketing alliance, the technology partner is completely dependent on the marketing partner's performance. If the exclusive marketing partner does not succeed in the marketplace, the technology partner suffers and has no other options. The concept of "earned exclusivity" deals with this problem by ensuring that the marketing partner meets specific performance metrics as a condition of continued exclusivity. In some situations, continued exclusivity is tied to a series of minimum payments to the technology partner. Such payments provide some protection to the technology partner from deliberate strategic slowdowns by the marketing partner. In those cases the payments are often referred to as "parking protection."

The Battelle Planning and Negotiating Team decided that the Strategic Exclusivity element in the MicroCATS alliance would probably involve a trade-off. The team wanted a balance between giving a head start to the oil company partner and Battelle's intent to provide the technology to the entire oil industry. The team recognized that the trade-off, which required a time period before the MicroCATS technology was broadly marketed, was closely coupled to the Financial Pie-Split element. For example, if the oil company partner had a share of the financial returns from broader marketing, then the partner would be encouraged to rapidly deploy the technology. The difficulty was in quantifying that trade-off. Since the Financial Pie-Split element was still to be developed, the team captured the basic idea of a trade-off in its stated position on this element. In step 3, Battelle needed to ensure that a prospective oil company partner was strategically aligned with the idea of ultimate wide availability to the industry.

Post-SAE Elements and Task Assignments

By the time the Battelle team had gone through all the SAEs, except Intersections, their energy was starting to flag. Wayne asked the team to spend the remaining time in the first meeting on post-SAE elements, such as Intellectual Property and Financial Pie-Split. Initial ideas on those elements were recorded. Before the meeting broke up, Wayne assigned specific follow-up tasks to individual team members, based on the team's work at the meeting. For example, Wayne asked Byron Sohovich to start creating a Financial Pie-Split model for the alliance, based on the initial financial ideas from the meeting and on the SAEs. The lawyers on the Planning and Negotiating Team were asked to start preparing material for the Intellectual Property element.

Results of a Long Hard Day. As they moved through each element, the team learned that Alliance Framework elements are interdependent. When members created a position on one element, they sometimes found that position in conflict with a position on another element. Some interelement conflicts were resolved during the first meeting. Some remained, and the conflicts were recorded on the flipcharts. At the end of the day, the conference room walls were covered with flipcharts.

As the last action during the first meeting, the team developed the list of stakeholders within Battelle whose input would be important to the continuing planning process. *Stakeholders* is a word that means different things to different people. In the Alliance Framework process, a stakeholder is any group that must budget resources for the alliance during the first twenty-four months of the relationship, and anyone who must approve the alliance before the firm can sign the alliance contract. The team agreed on how team members would communicate the planning status to each stakeholder in order to begin getting the required feedback.

Following the first meeting, the consultants converted the flipchart record into the first written version of the Alliance Framework. That version 1.0 was a thoughtful but incomplete eighteen-page document. Some SAEs were well thought out and agreed upon. Others were fuzzy, or reflected serious differences among team members. The elements past the SAEs contained just a few ideas. Wayne distributed version 1.0 to all team members and asked them to reflect on all the elements in preparation for the second team meeting.

Second and Third Team Meetings

Alliance Framework version 1.0 was the starting point for the Planning and Negotiating Team's work at its second meeting. After receiving version 1.0, team members had solicited input from stakeholders on difficult points. This helped them prepare for discussion on elements where there had been substantial disagreement during the first meeting. During the second meeting, some disagreements were resolved. Others remained. Team members presented status reports on the work chartered by Wayne after the first meeting, such as the Financial Pie-Split and Intellectual Property elements. The alliance consultants once again recorded the entire discussion on flipcharts.

Following the second meeting, Wayne issued version 2.0 of the Alliance Framework. Version 2.0 was more complete, with some elements still needing information or reflecting differences of opinion among team members. But the SAEs, the elements needed for step 3, were in fairly good shape. The team concentrated its energies on those SAEs, with most of the work on post-SAE elements being done offline by assigned team members. In addition to the Intellectual Property and Financial Pie-Split elements, intensive work began on the rest of the elements, such as Term and Termination and Working Process and Governance.

Intersections

Version 2.0 also included the final SAE, Intersections. Intersections are existing commitments whose terms will impact on the prospective alliance. For example, a firm may already have a contract with a distributor to market products inside the Boundaries. Or certain intellectual property being brought by a party may be constrained because of the terms of an existing license granted to a third party. The larger the company, the more likely there will be a potential problem. It is not uncommon for people in one part of a complex firm to encumber a corporate asset without the knowledge of other people who are attempting to plan and negotiate an alliance using that asset. Revealing these intersections late in negotiations is guaranteed to cause ill will between potential partners. In developing the Intersections element, Planning and Negotiation Teams must always contact the firm's legal and intellectual property organizations for input. Depending on the nature of the prospective alliance, other organizations such as purchasing, sales, and R&D may be important sources of information on existing commitments that may have an impact on the alliance.

The Intersections element required special attention in the Battelle alliance. Some MicroCATS technology was developed with United States Government funding. The government had certain rights, which were carefully described in the Intersections element and considered in other elements such as Intellectual Property and Strategic Exclusivity. Both Battelle management and the management team of the prospective oil company partners had to understand the impact of those reserved rights on the alliance.

By the end of the third meeting, the team was ready

to get stakeholder comments in a more systematic manner. To do that, the Planning and Negotiating Team revised version 2.0 to include the resolutions of their earlier disagreements on SAEs. They also included the first draft versions of post-SAE elements such as Financial Pie-Split and Intellectual Property. That revision, version 3.0, was a carefully drawn picture of the prospective MicroCATS alliance, as seen by the team prior to systematic discussions with potential partners. While the post-SAE elements still needed more work (some fleshing out would require intensive discussions with prospective partners), version 3.0 had enough detail to enable stakeholders to make judgments as to the impacts both on Battelle as a whole and on their own organizations. The team sent version 3.0 of the Alliance Framework to all stakeholders and followed up for their input.

Every manager on the stakeholder list was contacted and actively encouraged to disagree, challenge, and react to every element in version 3.0. Wayne was preparing to meet with potential partners. He was going to tell the oil companies that Battelle stakeholders were ready to focus their resources like a laser beam on the goals of this alliance. If someone did not agree that this deal was in Battelle's best interests or how their resources were going be used, the time to speak up was now.

The feedback from stakeholders was generally positive. Internal misunderstandings were exposed and resolved. In some cases, disagreements were escalated to Ben Maiden (Wayne's boss) and other top corporate executives for resolution. The open discussions among stakeholders led to a better understanding of how MicroCATS technology fit into the broader strategy of Battelle beyond the oil industry alliance.

The stakeholder feedback was incorporated into version 4.0 of the Alliance Framework. That version was as far as the Planning and Negotiating Team could go before starting step 3 (strategic fit assessment) discussions with potential partners. As pointed out in Chapter 1, iterations of the internal Alliance Framework document continue during discussions with potential partners. Since alliance formation is a two-way street, partner reactions and inputs must be part of the feedback loop in internal planning. Battelle's team reached that point with version 4.0.

Tips for Completing Step 2 of the Alliance Framework

When building internal consensus, remember to:

- Introduce the Planning and Negotiating Team to the Alliance Framework tool.
- Ensure team understanding of potential pitfalls such as path dependence, lack of internal consensus, and strategic disagreements.
- Concentrate first on the Strategic Assessment Elements (SAEs).
- Get early informal feedback from stakeholders.
- Start work on post-SAE elements.
- Get more systematic stakeholder feedback when the iterated Alliance Framework presents a reasonably clear picture of the prospective alliance.

CHAPTER 4

APPROACHING POTENTIAL PARTNERS: STRATEGIC FIT ASSESSMENT

Why do 70 percent of alliances fail? Most should never have been created in the first place. Absent a rigorous approach for evaluating an opportunity, executives commit scarce resources to low-probability relationships. Wrong partner, wrong project, with fuzzy objectives and inadequate links to strategy on both sides. Most executives don't even know they've fallen into the trap.

Step 3 of the Alliance Framework provides management with a process for approaching potential partners and evaluating the strategic fit between firms. While no process is perfect, this one has helped hundreds of managers walk away from low-quality deals or verify the value of high-quality deals. Step 3 also acknowledges the fact that no one knows when negotiations actually begin. Inexperienced managers believe that negotiations begin at step 6, the step labeled "Negotiating an Agreement." Veterans know that negotiations begin the moment one firm approaches another. Step 3 is more than a simple assessment. It is the beginning of the give-and-take that culminates in a deal. With that in mind, let's follow Battelle's Planning and Negotiating Team as they approach potential partners and make their final selection.

Battelle Takes Step 3

From Battelle's previous analysis and informal discussions with six oil companies, it was clear that four companies had the skills and resources needed to be potential partners. Or was it? Publicly available information only takes you so far. The Planning and Negotiating Team's perceptions of the four companies consisted of a mixture of one part fact, three parts hearsay, and a whole lot of hope based on what the team needed to succeed. Worse yet, facts and figures are not the only important issues. Battelle needed a company of people as excited about this project as they were. That assessment never shows up in a Dun and Bradstreet report.

The team made the decision to approach all four potential partners simultaneously and let each one know that they were looking at more than one firm at a time. The team's work on the Strategic Assessment Elements

(SAEs) showed that the resource requirements of the alliance would likely require the participation of more than one oil company. Each oil company had to be informed that Battelle was thinking of a multiparty alliance and was talking to a number of companies in order to put together the right mix of resources. Approaching all four oil companies in parallel would enable Battelle to create that right mix with the right partners and shorten the time required to put the alliance together.

There was a touch of desperation in the team meeting that morning. The previous evening, Wayne Simmons gave Battelle's Investment Committee a progress report. The Investment Committee was made up of Battelle's most senior executives and was Wayne's version of a venture capitalist. Battelle sets aside a limited amount of money to fund high-priority ventures, and Wayne was using more than his share. The committee pushed hard with familiar questions: How soon will the team generate external funding? How much progress has been made in the scale-up program? When will you approach the most promising partners? Wayne's answers were familiar, too: "Soon." Wayne left the meeting with this admonition: three more months of funding unless he could line up partners to help.

With a ninety-day deadline, the Planning and Negotiating Team prepared for their first approach. Fortunately, they were not starting from scratch. Years ago, Wayne worked for a major oil company and knew key technical people in many oil industry firms. In recent months, Wayne and Laura Silva held informal meetings with people in six possible partner firms. They picked these six based on their knowledge of the industry and the firms' participation in technical forums on processing in

MAKING THE FIRST APPROACH TO POTENTIAL PARTNERS

Often, companies are uncertain how to approach potential partners. Battelle had existing relevant contacts in the oil industry. But what can be done in situations where prior contacts are inadequate for an approach? Industry associations, professional societies, and law and accounting firms can sometimes facilitate introductions. One of the best, but often overlooked, ways to initiate contacts is through a potential partner's business development or licensing office. Most business development and licensing managers in a wide variety of industries belong to the Licensing Executives Society (LES). Anyone interested in alliances, business development, and licensing should consider joining this organization (*www.usa-canada.les.org*). LES members are well connected to the right people within their firms who must be involved in discussing any specific alliance opportunity.

If the potential partner firm does not have a business development group, another approach point is the relevant business unit head. This person will have the profit/loss responsibility for any alliance activity and is therefore well positioned to make early decisions.

If the product or service in question has a strong technology base, a third approach point is the chief technology officer of the potential partner firm. When the technology is of interest, this person often becomes an early champion of the proposed alliance.

remote locations. In the informal meetings, Wayne and Laura were careful not to disclose, or receive, any proprietary information. They described, in broad terms, the possible use of MicroCATS technology in the oil industry. The informal meetings gave Battelle a sense of each firm's capabilities and interest level in a cooperative MicroCATS project. It also gave Wayne and Laura insights into the organizational structure and decision-making process of each company. The informal meetings enabled them to disqualify two companies from further consideration, leaving four on the short list of potential partners.

──────

How does your firm approach potential alliance partners?

──────

There was another serious problem. The nature of the issues being discussed required that oil company senior managers and key stakeholders participate in future discussions. Anything less would add months to the planning and negotiation cycle, months the Battelle team did not have. Why these high-level people? Only they could make the required strategic decisions, agree on devoting resources to planning and negotiating the alliance, and reassign people from other projects onto a planning team. For the alliance formation process to move ahead quickly, key stakeholders inside each company had to buy in to the alliance concept. But how could Battelle's team convince them to attend? These were busy people with businesses to run. Wayne could imagine their reactions: "Who is Battelle?" "What do they know about production or petrochemical manufacturing?" "I've been in the oil business my entire career and I've never seen Battelle in the oil patch." This was a problem.

After discussion, Battelle's Planning and Negotiating Team decided on a four-phase process for approaching the four short-list candidates and conducting strategic fit assessments:

1. The team would meet with Wayne and Laura's prior contacts and work with those contacts to identify an appropriate mix of senior people and key stakeholders from both Battelle and the oil company. The goal was to have all of the important stakeholder groups at the meetings.

2. The team would conduct separate meetings with all four oil companies over a short time period. In each meeting, Wayne and his team would explain the Alliance Framework and its elements, define the Strategic Assessment Elements for the prospective alliance, and describe Battelle's position on each of the SAEs. Wayne would also propose a process and timetables for going forward with both the strategic fit assessment (step 3) and the resource fit assessment (step 4). At this first meeting, Battelle did not expect a firm reaction from the oil company, just a full hearing of the idea. Battelle would let each oil company know that it was presenting the alliance idea to other firms. Beyond the obvious integrity issue and the need to disclose the possibility of a multiparty alliance, the team thought that knowing more than one oil company was involved would stimulate each firm to move quickly on the strategic fit and resource fit assessments.

3. Following the first meeting, Battelle would provide each oil company with a complete written state-

ment of its positions on the SAEs. That would help oil company attendees to discuss Battelle's vision internally among other senior managers and all other stakeholders. It would also allow oil company management to better formulate their responses.

4. As soon as possible after the first meeting, Battelle and each oil company would meet again. At that meeting, Battelle and the prospective partner would determine whether they were sufficiently aligned on the SAEs to move ahead to step 4: resource fit assessment.

This straightforward approach met both sides' needs. The complexity of the alliance required giving the oil companies an opportunity to reflect on Battelle's SAE positions. The size of the oil companies' internal organizations required that senior-level executives attend. The follow-up senior management meeting provided some level of comfort that the project was a high priority in each oil company. This priority assessment was vital. The Planning and Negotiating Team knew that agreement on the SAEs did not fully reveal an oil company's view of the project's importance. Battelle's top management was behind this project, and Battelle's R&D staff was dedicated to success. The oil companies, however, were large firms with many internal power centers and complex decision-making processes. Only senior people in each oil company could determine the priority of this alliance relative to other projects.

Armed with Battelle's positions on the SAEs, the assurance of a substantive presentation, and the promise of solving some of the pressing issues in the oil business, Wayne and Laura were ready for their first high-level meetings with the four potential partners.

The First Meetings

Prior to each meeting, lawyers for Battelle and the oil company drafted an appropriate nondisclosure agreement (NDA) that clearly described the rules for the use of information shared during the meetings. Wayne and Laura provided their contacts with advance information on the Alliance Framework tool, Battelle's list of the relevant SAEs for this alliance, and a brief summary of Battelle's positions on each SAE. The contacts circulated that material in advance to meeting participants.

In accordance with the agreement reached between Wayne and his oil company contacts, each meeting was led either by Wayne and his oil company counterpart or by executives at higher corporate levels. Wayne, Laura, and other Battelle team members participated in all the meetings, as did Wayne's contacts and other representatives of oil company stakeholder groups, such as R&D and production engineering.

Every good meeting has an agenda, and these meetings were no exception. The agenda in Figure 4-1 kept each meeting on track and on time.

Here's how a typical initial meeting worked for Battelle. After an overview of the opportunity, Wayne described the Alliance Framework tool and each of its elements, emphasizing the value of SAEs in assessing strategic fit.

He reviewed Battelle's proposed process for partner selection, and followed up with a description of Battelle's positions on the SAEs. These positions were not presented as "take it or leave it." Rather, the oil company participants were encouraged to ask questions and comment on Battelle's positions, without necessarily reacting firmly on the spot. Wayne emphasized that the Battelle team was

Figure 4-1. Meeting agenda for Battelle's first approach to a potential partner.

- Introductions
- Battelle's view of the marketplace opportunity
- Description of the Alliance Framework and its elements
- Detailed discussion of the Strategic Assessment Elements (SAEs) and their use in selecting a partner and assessing strategic fit
- An overview of Battelle's positions on each SAE (a summary of Battelle's version 4.0 Alliance Framework)
- Battelle Intersections
- Questions and answers
- Team memberships
- Next steps
- Adjourn

not asking for a decision to go forward with the alliance formation process at this first meeting. It was asking for a chance to present Battelle's view of the opportunity the alliance posed and to answer any questions.

In the next agenda item, Laura explained that an intersection is a situation in either firm that would constrain the alliance, even if both firms successfully completed the negotiation. She reminded everyone that this is a particularly insidious problem inside a large firm, where the company may have made conflicting commitments that are not widely known throughout the organization. Laura described Battelle's one intersection: Since specific technical inputs to MicroCATS were developed at the Pacific Northwest National Laboratory with federal funding, the government had certain rights to use the technology. Laura clearly explained the impact of those government rights on the project.

She suggested that the oil company executives look for intersections of their own in at least four places:

- The legal department, because they know about conflicting contracts
- The intellectual property (IP) organization, because they know about constraints on intellectual assets
- The purchasing department, because those people know everything
- Top corporate management, because if a conflicting deal was currently under negotiation, top management would know about it

In all four meetings, it appeared that the oil company executives were interested. However, the oil companies needed time to consider Battelle's proposal. Wayne outlined a schedule for next steps, including additional discussion of SAEs, mutual determination of strategic fit, and possible resource evaluations. He emphasized the fact that alliance planning and negotiating consumes management time and travel budgets. Trying to coordinate peoples' schedules is a nightmare, particularly when the people who must be engaged are busy with other things. Battelle and the oil company executives had to understand what those resource demands are likely to be, and they must be willing to commit those resources to the alliance formation process. Therefore, Wayne suggested a timeline consistent with Battelle's three-month schedule.

One of the last items in the first meeting with each oil company was a discussion of team membership. Wayne's introduction of the Alliance Framework included the idea that when one firm appoints a Planning and Negotiating Team led by a line manager and the other firm appoints a lawyer and a business development expert, alliance discussions start off in a failure mode. Wayne encouraged the oil company executives to appoint a team complementary to Battelle's. Wayne described the reasons behind Battelle's selection of team members, pointing out that the team represented all key internal stakeholders and was supported by alliance experts. Wayne's argument was persuasive, and each prospective partner appointed an appropriate team that included relevant stakeholders and alliance specialists.

Review your firm's agendas for first meetings with prospective partners. Should anything be added?

First Meeting Follow-Ups

The Alliance Framework process was paying off for Battelle. The SAEs surfaced strategic disagreements with each company. Battelle worked on the disagreements with each firm separately and was able to resolve them.

The Planning and Negotiating Team realized that going on to step 4, resource fit assessment, and further steps with just one oil company would consume their limited resources. This prompted the team to focus attention on the most likely partner first. The strategy was to reach an agreement with that company and then complete the Alliance Framework process with the other firms. Not only did this strategy allow Battelle to focus its resources, it also successfully set the stage for the subsequent deals. The first agreement became the template for agreements with two other oil company partners, ensuring compatibility among the individual agreements in an alliance among Battelle and three oil company partners. The fourth potential partner dropped out during step 4, resource fit assessment, which we will discuss in the next chapter.

INTRODUCING THE ALLIANCE FRAMEWORK TO THE PARTNER

What should you do if the potential partner does not know about the Alliance Framework or is reluctant to use it? It depends on the nature of the partner. Some firms have their own version of an alliance creation process. As long as that creation process covers the key issues of gaining internal consensus, bringing all key stakeholders onto the alliance Planning and Negotiating Team, and linking the alliance formation process to strategy, it should be an acceptable alternative to the Alliance Framework.

A challenge arises when the potential partner has no effective internal alliance formation process. In our experience, the best path forward is to introduce the Alliance Framework in the course of describing the alliance concept to each potential partner during the early stages of step 3, strategic fit assessment. The details of how that introduction is done depend on circumstances and the styles of managers on both sides. Even with a very brief Alliance Framework overview presented at a first meeting, a prospective partner with no Alliance Framework experience will learn a great deal about the SAEs as you present your point of view on each element. If your firm makes a more complete Alliance Framework presentation, a prospective partner will get a clearer understanding of the entire process and the significance of all Alliance Framework elements. Sometimes a more thorough presentation is deferred until a follow-up meeting, after the partner reflects on the value of using the Alliance Framework tool in their own internal planning process, based on the brief overview in a first meeting.

In any event, the Alliance Framework is never presented as a "you must use this technique" ultimatum, but rather as a way to show the partner what process your firm uses. In all cases, your firm must be sensitive to the partner's alliance experience and management style. In practice, we find that when a prospective partner does not already have a well-thought-out internal process to plan and negotiate alliances, they often adopt the Alliance Framework.

What if you perceive that a prospective partner does not intend to use a systematic planning process? Your firm has assured the prospective partner that you are using a process to expose and resolve internal disagreements. Your firm must understand how the partner intends to address these issues, and you need to be satisfied that unresolved disagreements on the other side will not sink the alliance during implementation. Your perception that a prospective partner may not be dealing effectively with internal disagreements on their side of the deal could lead to disqualification of that partner.

Tips for Completing Step 3 of the Alliance Framework

When approaching potential partners:

- Set up your step 3 meetings with the right people on both sides, and have carefully planned agendas.
- Introduce the Alliance Framework at the level of detail appropriate to the circumstances.
- Use the Strategic Assessment Elements (SAEs) to introduce the alliance concept and determine strategic fit.
- Determine if a prospective partner will be able to properly develop its internal alliances, either through the use of the Alliance Framework or alternative methods.
- Persuade the partner to appoint a complementary Planning and Negotiating Team.

CHAPTER 5

CONDUCTING THE RESOURCE FIT ASSESSMENT

In step 3 of the Alliance Framework process, we focused on assessing whether prospective alliance partners are strategically aligned. During step 4, resource fit assessment, we need to determine the extent to which potential partners bring the complementary resources required for successful implementation. Too often, firms join forces only to find that each had overly optimistic expectations of the other's skill sets and resources. That optimism turns to pessimism after the deal is signed and one or both firms discover gaps in the other's capabilities. Resource fit assessment is designed to deal with this issue. It must be based on a well-planned and open exchange of information, in both directions, about both firms' relevant capabilities. Invariably, the exchange involves discussions among functional experts in both firms, and usually includes on-site visits to facilities such as laboratories, factories, or sales offices. These discussions and reciprocal visits held during step 4 are referred to as "Tirekicks."

It is not surprising that firms have difficulty gauging the quality and quantity of a potential partner's resources. Resource fit assessment is time-consuming and subjective. Some resources, such as physical plants, lend themselves to effective evaluation. Others, such as know-how and trade secrets, are tougher to assess. Step 4 is further complicated by the need for managers to judge the firms' abilities to effectively combine and deploy their resources. For example, even if both firms respect the others' R&D capabilities, managers must make an additional judgment as to how well the R&D staffs will work together.

Resource Fit Assessment Follows Strategic Fit Assessment for Good Reasons

Resource fit assessment should begin only after the assessment of strategic fit is complete. Why? Tirekicks consume considerable time and energy and often involve many people in both firms beyond Planning and Negotiating Team members. If the Strategic Assessment Elements (SAEs) show that two companies do not fit strategically, there is no reason to waste resources on Tirekicks.

Completing strategic fit assessment first is also a risk management tool. The potential for undue exposure to the partner's proprietary information increases significantly during Tirekicks. Taking these risks is pointless if the firms do not fit strategically.

Finally, information generated during strategic fit assessment is an important input into planning Tirekicks. During strategic fit assessment, much is learned about what each company is expected to bring into the alliance. The Roles element outlines "who will do what." The Overall Resources element specifies "who will bring what" to the alliance. These two elements help both Planning and Negotiating Teams focus on the right areas during Tirekicks. For example, if two firms in a potential alliance agree in step 3 that Company A will carry out the mechanical design of a jointly developed product, then in step 4, Company B must assess Company A's mechanical design capability. If during discussion of the SAEs the firms are uncertain on who should carry out that Role, the Tirekicks will help answer the question by allowing each firm to assess the other's ability to provide those resources.

Tools for Mitigating Tirekick Risks

Tirekicks pose risks to both sides. The inherent risks in sharing intellectual property increases significantly during Tirekicks. Since the parties have not signed an alliance agreement, each party's proprietary information must be protected if the deal falls through. The keys to success are the careful planning and negotiating of Tirekick agendas and well-crafted nondisclosure agreements.

TIREKICKS VS. "DUE DILIGENCE"

While the Tirekick concept may appear to resemble a due diligence process, its purpose and timing is fundamentally different. Tirekicks are carried out early in the alliance formation process, as one of the two steps needed to select a potential partner for detailed negotiations. Tirekicks look in-depth at resource fit as seen by competent experts on both sides. Due diligence, which is usually carried out later in the alliance formation process, should be focused on confirming representations made during the negotiations, such as the validity of a partner's statements about its existing intellectual property rights. Depending on circumstances, some due diligence activities could occur early on, but their purposes are quite distinct from the purposes of Tirekicks. Let's use some examples to illustrate due diligence.

Suppose, during step 3 (strategic fit assessment), our firm and a prospective partner agree in the Overall Resources element that the partner will contribute a key patent licensed from a third-party inventor. However, it becomes apparent in step 3 that the terms of the licensing agreement between the partner and this third party will have an important impact on the partner's alliance with our firm. For example, our firm does not want the third-party inventor to have any rights to inventions coming out of the work in the alliance between our firm and our partner. Because of that, the strategic fit of this potential partner depends strongly on the terms of that license. While the partner assures us that there will be no problems, our intellectual property counsel remains concerned. Our firm insists on reviewing the licensing agreement, as a due diligence action. Will the prospective partner permit that review as part of step 3, or will the partner ask us to wait until later in the Alliance Framework process? That depends on the dynamics of the negotiation and the risks that our firm is willing to take in going forward to subsequent steps without reviewing the in-license agreement. In any event, the Alliance Framework process has revealed a due diligence issue in step 3 that must be addressed before step 6 (negotiating an agreement) is completed with this potential partner.

In another example, during step 6, our firm agrees to fund specific development work done by a small start-up firm, as part of the Financial Pie-Split element. Although the prospective partner assures us that it uses "generally accepted accounting principles" in calculating development costs, we are aware that cost calculation methods vary widely among firms. Furthermore, our firm is concerned about the start-up's financial viability and whether our payments might be used for other purposes if the partner had trouble paying its bills. Both of these issues lead us to ask for a financial audit of the partner before completing step 6.

Occasionally, due diligence is not connected to a specific alliance issue. For example, a prominent consumer-products firm might be concerned about a potential partner's environmental problems. While the focus of the prospective alliance has nothing to do with environmental issues, the consumer-products firm may be worried about the potential for bad publicity caused by an alliance with a perceived "polluter." For that reason, the consumer-products firm may ask for a review of environmental issues faced by the partner.

Tirekick Agendas and the Asset Map

Tirekick agendas must enable each firm to learn enough to carry out effective resource fit assessment while minimizing the risks of overdisclosure.

Thinking through Tirekick agendas is a valuable exercise for internal stakeholders. This is the first time each stakeholder must think through the specific resources required from the partner and develop a strategy for evaluating those resources. When the alliance focuses on a product or service that is well understood by both firms, Tirekicks can be relatively straightforward. Each side is familiar with the resources that must be combined. When the alliance focuses on an area new to one or both partners, Tirekicks are far more difficult, because each side must predict what resources are needed and develop methods for their assessment. In either situation, Tirekicks require both firms to focus on the fundamental resource needs of the alliance.

Two tools help both sides plan and negotiate Tirekick agendas: the Asset Map and the Tirekick Matrix. The Asset Map addresses four interrelated questions:

1. What does each firm need to learn about the other's capabilities?
2. What is each willing not to learn?
3. What is each firm willing to reveal?
4. What is each not willing to reveal?

The Asset Map must cover these four questions in enough detail so that both firms have a clear understanding of what will—and won't—be revealed.

Each firm fills out the Asset Map twice, once from its perspective and once from the partner's perspective (see

Figures 5-1 and 5-2). Sharing the Asset Maps with the partner acts as a vital check before Tirekicks begin so that both partners know whether they agree on the information to be exchanged and the limitations on exposure. Since the Asset Map identifies resources to be assessed at a detailed level, both firms will get a clear understanding of the other's expectations for the Tirekicks and will be able to negotiate mutually acceptable agendas.

Figure 5-1. Asset Map (our firm).

- What must we learn about the partner's capabilities?
    - a)
    - b)
    - c)
- What are we willing not to learn?
    - a)
    - b)
    - c)
- What are we willing to reveal to the partner?
    - a)
    - b)
    - c)
- What are we not willing to reveal?
    - a)
    - b)
    - c)

Figure 5-2. Asset Map (partner firm).

- What must the partner learn about our capabilities?
  - a)
  - b)
  - c)
- What are they willing not to learn?
  - a)
  - b)
  - c)
- What are they willing to show us?
  - a)
  - b)
  - c)
- What are they not willing to show us?
  - a)
  - b)
  - c)

The Tirekick Matrix

The Tirekick Matrix complements the Asset Maps by addressing the logistics of the Tirekicks: Who will participate on both sides? Where and how will the Tirekicks be carried out? The Tirekick Matrix (see Figure 5-3) helps companies answer these questions quickly and efficiently. Once again, each company fills out the Tirekick Matrix twice, once for itself and once for the partner.

Figure 5-3. Tirekick Matrix.

	Asset 1	Asset 2	Asset 3
Responsible manager, sending firm			
Responsible manager, receiving firm			
Employees, sending firm			
Employees, receiving firm			
Where and how assessment will be carried out			

What process does your firm use to determine what resources must be evaluated? How do you come to agreement with the potential partner?

Using the Asset Map as input, the Tirekick Matrix describes what resources the firm has agreed to reveal to the partner. Those resources are detailed along the horizontal axis of Figure 5-3. The vertical axis outlines how the Tirekicks will be carried out. For example, the rows "Responsible manager, sending firm" and "Responsible manager, receiving firm" identify the managers in charge of the evaluation of each specific resource, on both sides. The rows "Employees, sending firm" and "Employees, receiving firm" identify the specific employees who will participate in the evaluation on both sides. Agreement on the number and identification of individuals will help to eliminate a common complaint of small firms in large company/small company alliances. As one manager put it:

> When our potential partner came to look at our facility, they came in a bus. When the stream of people finally stopped, we realized that they brought more people than we had employees. I wanted to put them to work, but our [company] president said that was impolite.

The row labeled "Where and How" ensures that both parties have similar expectations of where the Tirekick will take place and how the evaluation will be carried out. For example, suppose one firm wants to evaluate a potential partner's new chemical process innovation. Will one scientist conduct a one-hour presentation in a conference room, or will ten scientists from the interested firm visit the laboratory? If so, what will those scientists see?

———

Think back to your last Tirekick visit: Was the potential partner prepared for how you were going to evaluate their resources? Did you learn what you needed to know?

———

The Asset Map and the Tirekick Matrix are interrelated. For example, the "Where and How" row in the Tirekick Matrix is closely connected to the "What do we need to learn" and "What are you willing to reveal" aspects of the Asset Map. Coming to agreement on both issues in advance of the Tirekick meetings helps both firms conduct an effective resource fit assessment.

Properly planned Tirekicks provide important fringe benefits to both firms. People on both sides get to know each other, during the working day and often over dinner or other social events. Since Tirekicks are held after strategic fit assessment and before negotiations on all other Alliance Framework elements, team members have the opportunity to break down personal barriers before beginning the hard work of negotiating the remaining elements. Just as important, stakeholders who will work together during implementation have the opportunity to develop personal contacts and mutual respect before implementation begins. Tirekick planning should ensure that these fringe benefits are achieved through the proper choice of Tirekick participants.

Nondisclosure Agreements

The sensitivity of the issues being discussed during alliance negotiations requires a carefully written agreement protecting the proprietary information of both firms. That agreement is usually called a nondisclosure agreement (NDA) or confidentiality agreement.

An NDA deals with the sharing of proprietary information such as business plans, marketing insights and data, and technical advances not yet made public. The alliance agreement reached at the end of successful negotiations will contain provisions dealing with these matters. In contrast, the NDA covers the periods before the potential partners have formed an alliance and after negotiations break off, if an alliance contract is not reached. The "rules of the road" in an NDA may be quite different from the rules in an alliance agreement.

Managers responsible for alliance planning and negotiations should be aware of two common aspects of NDAs that affect steps 3 and 4:

- *Confidentiality Requirement.* The first aspect describes the responsibilities of each firm to protect information learned from the other from disclosure to unauthorized persons. This confidentiality requirement usually restricts disclosure outside the receiving firm, and sometimes restricts disclosure beyond a specific group of people inside the receiving firm. Most NDAs specify a time period for confidentiality and provide for exceptions, such as information that becomes publicly known through no fault of the receiving party.

- *Restrictions on Use.* The second aspect deals with the allowed use of received information, frequently restricting the use of the information to the negotiation of the potential alliance. The restrictions on use sometimes allow for exceptions, such as a party's right to use the same information if independently developed by that party.

It is essential to follow the guidance of experienced legal counsel in preparing an NDA that fits the specific circumstances of your alliance.

The negotiation of an NDA involves reaching a mutually satisfactory balance between each firm's need to protect its proprietary information and the conflicting needs to avoid being blocked from certain activities and being unduly burdened with mechanisms to protect information. Here are two examples to illustrate the balance problem, although NDAs often present other problems as well.

- *Limitations on Sharing Information Internally.* In Chapters 1 and 2, we emphasized the need to share alliance planning broadly among all stakeholders inside the firm. That need could conflict with an NDA that calls for limited internal distribution of information received from a potential partner. Excessively tight limits in an NDA might prevent the sharing of Tirekick results among stakeholders, limiting the firm's ability to evaluate resource fit and damaging the development of the internal alliances discussed in Chapter 1. For that reason, limitations on internal distribution must be carefully drafted to permit disclosure to appropriate stakeholders on both sides.

- *Limitations on the Use of Received Information.* Another potential conflict arises from provisions that limit use of received information. Suppose my firm receives information from yours on the results of consumer interest in a potential new product. If I am prohibited from using that information except to consider a possible development alliance for that product, I may be impeded from pursuing that new product if we do not form an alliance. I may have to demonstrate that I did not use your information in deciding to develop the product, a burden that may be very difficult to overcome. This is an example of "embedding," a situation in which it becomes difficult for one side to avoid using information received from the other side. There are many solutions to this type of problem, depending on the specific circumstances. Embedding is discussed further under the Intellectual Property element in Chapter 8.

Many managers treat the NDA as routine boilerplate and do not understand the potential for adverse consequences. Those managers may execute a "standard" NDA sent to them by a prospective partner without consulting their own counsel or considering the impact of NDA provisions on their specific situation. A well-crafted NDA allows both parties to effectively conduct steps 3 and 4. However, developing that agreement requires a bit of concentrated effort among Planning and Negotiating Team Leaders and lawyers for both sides.

Let's look at an example of well-planned and executed Tirekicks that led to an important successful alliance: the AT&T Microelectronics/NEC CMOS joint development alliance.

AT&T Microelectronics/NEC CMOS Alliance

CMOS (complementary metal oxide semiconductor) is the fundamental semiconductor chip technology used to make many of the most important semiconductor products, including memory and logic devices. Alliances among competitors were not new in the semiconductor chip industry in the late 1980s, when AT&T Microelectronics and NEC* began thinking about an alliance to jointly develop new generations of CMOS technology. However, most alliances among competitors

---

*AT&T Microelectronics became Lucent Microelectronics in 1995 and was spun off as Agere Systems in 2001. NEC spun off its microelectronics business as NEC Electronics Corporation in 2002.

were focused on specific products or on a single scientific area. For example, a semiconductor firm might provide a limited license to a competitor for a specific chip design to meet customer demands for multiple sources of chip supply. Two firms might agree to combine scientific resources to conduct joint long-term research with an uncertain payoff. However, the prospective AT&T Microelectronics/NEC alliance was different. Two competing firms were going to combine resources to develop important near-term underlying technology. Both AT&T Microelectronics and NEC would have to deal with the prospects of revealing important proprietary knowledge to a competitor, and seeing that competitor use jointly developed technology in the marketplace.

Direct competitive rivalry in the integrated circuit market was not the only problem. There were broader competitive, political, and cultural gulfs between the two companies. NEC (as the Nippon Electric Company, Limited) had been established near the end of the nineteenth century as a joint venture with Western Electric, which at that time was AT&T's manufacturing arm. Over the decades, and especially after Japan's post–World War II economic rebirth, NEC and AT&T had become competitors across a wide range of products. For example, they competed in supplying telecommunications equipment to telephone companies around the world, including those in each other's home markets.

In addition, during the 1980s the governments of the United States and Japan were engaged in a series of trade disputes with the semiconductor chip business taking center stage. The United States claimed that Japan had unfairly limited market access to U.S.-based chip suppliers. The U.S. chipmakers were mostly supportive of their government's efforts to open the market, while Japanese chipmakers were understandably concerned over governmental pressure to share their markets with newcomers.

Strained relationships could be found at many levels within each company. Some U.S. executives resented what they viewed as unfair Japanese exploitation of knowledge freely (and, as some felt, naively) shared with visiting Japanese scientists and engineers. On their side, some leaders in the Japanese chip industry felt that U.S. companies had lost their dominant industry position through complacency and lack of attention to customer needs. Middle managers and technical staffs in both countries shared those attitudes, so the professional interactions among scientists and engineers were guarded.

All of these issues were compounded by a lack of strong interpersonal relationships between key people in AT&T Microelectronics and NEC who would have to work together on the project. Since those people had not previously worked together, feelings of mutual trust had not yet developed. All of these factors made resource fit assessment especially challenging for the AT&T Microelectronics/NEC alliance.

Informal resource fit assessments started when senior executives in both firms decided that an alliance might be in their future. Both firms used public information, industry knowledge, and past interactions to develop perceptions of the other's capabilities. However, no one knew how accurate these perceptions really were. Industry knowledge is always incomplete and subject to interpretation. Past interactions are only relevant if they are with the same groups and people who will work in the alliance. In the final analysis, the only way that NEC and AT&T executives could satisfy themselves that their resources fit together for the CMOS project was to conduct systematic Tirekicks.

During the earlier strategic fit assessment, AT&T Microelectronics and NEC executives understood that Tirekicks would require several multiday meetings of the technical staffs, both at AT&T's Bell Labs facilities in New Jersey and Pennsylvania and at NEC's laboratories outside Tokyo. Because of the importance of CMOS technology to both firms, the sensitivity of the relevant scientific information, and the competitive relationship between the companies, the executives recognized that the Tirekick agendas required careful planning. The AT&T Team Leader and his top technical and alliance advisers went to Tokyo specifically to negotiate Tirekick agendas with their NEC counterparts.

During the agenda negotiations, both sides knew that the possible alliance required a clear understanding of how far the other laboratory had gone in research on next-generation CMOS technology. For every technical area, such as materials, chemical processes, and pattern generation, the firms agreed on the details of what scientific information would be disclosed and what would be held back. Both sides were satisfied that the level of disclosure would enable adequate evaluation of the status of the other's CMOS R&D program and how that program compared to their own. They also agreed on the people who would be involved in Tirekick meetings, knowing that both sides wanted to evaluate the capabilities of each other's key technical staff and how well the two staffs would work together. Beyond those issues, the agendas also included both firms' future CMOS scientific directions. If the scientific goals were too far apart, a collaborative effort would never succeed. Finally, the two firms negotiated a suitable nondisclosure agreement to cover the Tirekicks.

Tirekicks in the United States and Japan

AT&T Microelectronics management decided to put the Bell Labs scientists and engineers through a cultural orientation before the first Tirekick visit to NEC. Some of the Bell Labs people had been to professional society meetings in Japan and had discussed technical issues with Japanese counterparts. But few knew Japanese people on a personal level, and none had experienced the type of in-depth interactions that the Tirekicks would require. The cultural training covered Japanese customs, such as bringing suitable gifts for hosts and the reluctance to use first names with anyone but family and intimate friends. The training went beyond social customs to matters that would directly impact on the Tirekick process, such as Japanese methods of consensus building in making important decisions.

The Tirekicks went even better than expected. NEC scientists spent several days at AT&T's laboratories in New Jersey and Pennsylvania, listening to Bell Labs scientists describe the state of their R&D program. Bell Labs invited the NEC people into its laboratories for some hands-on exposure. There were a few bad moments, such as when an NEC scientist asked an important question that a Bell Labs scientist balked at answering. But the Team Leaders and the others who had participated in the agenda negotiations were able to deal with those problems on the spot, based on the prior understandings reached in the Tokyo meeting.

During the return visits to Japan, NEC treated the Bell Labs people exactly the same way. There were rough spots, just as in the visits to the United States. For example, the first Tokyo meeting did not anticipate every discrepancy between what Bell Labs people wanted to know and what NEC was willing to reveal. The working relationships previously established between the Team Leaders again paid off, as they were able to quickly resolve the problems.

Both companies achieved their Tirekick objectives. Enough information was exchanged to convince both firms' scientists that the two R&D programs were compatible. Beyond that, the discussions set the stage for the later negotiation of the details of the joint development program.

The scientific interchanges also dispelled initial concerns on both sides about the quality of the other firm's staff. The Bell Labs staff found that they had more in common with their NEC counterparts than they had anticipated. Both groups had similar advanced educations, and they shared scientific values. Many people in both companies had traveled widely and had common scientific contacts around the world. Most important, Bell Labs and NEC personnel found that they shared certain other characteristics, such as an interest in listening carefully and courteously to the other's views.

Judy Sheft, the lead negotiator for AT&T, emphasizes the fringe benefits of the Tirekick process:

> **In the evenings, scientists and engineers from Bell Labs and NEC were able to break the ice and informally discuss such matters as differences in management styles in the two organizations and how those style differences might be resolved during the alliance. Looking back at the subsequent years of successful alliance implementation, I realize that the close working relationships between NEC and Bell Labs had their genesis in places like certain karaoke bars in Tokyo.**

Based on the successful Tirekicks, AT&T Microelectronics and NEC went on to negotiate and implement a highly successful alliance in which the firms jointly developed new CMOS technology that both used in their own manufacture of many important products. The lessons from those Tirekicks are powerful. Tirekicks require a negotiation and an implementation process all their own. The rigor firms must infuse into resource fit assessment goes beyond simple observation. It requires partners to understand their own needs in-depth and to possess the skills to evaluate the other firm's assets against the demands of those needs. The value of Tirekicks extends beyond an assessment of resource fit. They are the first opportunity to develop the interpersonal relationships that are so important to alliance success.

Tips for Completing Step 4 of the Alliance Framework

When conducting a resource fit assessment, remember to:

- Carefully plan and negotiate Tirekick agendas, with the aid of the Asset Map and Tirekick Matrix tools.
- Have corporate counsel properly craft a Nondisclosure Agreement (NDA).
- Ensure all employees understand the NDA and their responsibilities related to nondisclosure.
- Carry out cultural orientations when needed.
- Exploit the fringe benefits of developing interpersonal relationships.

SELECTING THE PARTNER

Alliances are often compared to marriages. Sometimes the analogy holds, other times it does not. But there is one way in which the analogy holds perfectly. In alliances, as in marriages, there is no recovery from selecting the wrong spouse. The stories of companies selecting the wrong partner are legendary. In one case, a small firm developed a medical diagnostic test for the physician's office. With no marketing or sales force of its own, the firm formed an alliance with a major medical diagnostic company. However, the large firm's sales force was focused on the centralized laboratories of hospitals and diagnostic centers, with no presence in the doctors' office. The result? Very disappointing sales.

The partner selection process, which is step 5 of the Alliance Framework, boils down to three issues:

1. Which potential partner presents the least trouble-some disagreements in Strategic Assessment Elements (SAEs), to be resolved in step 6 final negotiations?
2. Which potential partner provides the best match of required resources?
3. Which potential partner has self-selected itself into the deal?

In an ideal world, the optimum partner is obvious after steps 3 and 4. In the real world, narrowing down the list to one partner, or a select few, can be a messy business. It is rare that a single potential partner is completely aligned on all SAEs or brings all the needed complementary resources. More often, each potential partner disagrees with the firm's position on one or more SAEs in step 3 (strategic fit assessment). The quality and quantity of required resources, as revealed in step 4 (resource fit assessment), varies among potential partners, and sometimes every potential partner is missing one or more of those resources. The level of partner commitment to alliance objectives is also an open question that requires Planning and Negotiating Team judgment. In this chapter we will discuss how the firm can use the Alliance Framework to make the best possible choice of potential partners and move ahead to negotiating an agreement in step 6.

Looping Back to Step 2, Achieving Internal Consensus

The strategic fit and resource fit assessments provide a great deal of hard information about each partner. It is clear where the strategic interests of the firms come together and where they diverge. The Planning and Negotiating Team also understands the quality and quantity of each partner's resources. Armed with this information, the team loops back to step 2 and begins the process of resolving SAE conflicts and resource shortfalls.

The Strategic Fit Reconciliation Map

There are three possibilities in dealing with SAE disagreements:

1. Agree with the partner's position.
2. Convince the partner to agree to your position.
3. Develop a compromise between the two positions.

The Strategic Fit Reconciliation Map moves this process along by providing a visual summary of the strategic fit between each partner. It guides the team's thinking on resolving SAE conflicts. It also acts as a communication tool for top corporate management by allowing them to assess the strategic fit between the firms "at a glance."

The Strategic Fit Reconciliation Map is a simple matrix, shown in blank form in Figure 6-1. The SAEs used in steps 2 and 3 make up the vertical axis. Potential partners are identified on the horizontal axis.

As the Planning and Negotiating Team loops back to step 2 in its efforts to deal with SAE conflicts, they update the Strategic Fit Reconciliation Map to reflect current thinking. For example, consider the case of a large pet food company using an alliance to incorporate novel nutritional ingredients into its pet foods. The goal of the alliance is to jointly develop a series of new products with

Figure 6-1. Strategic Fit Reconciliation Map.

Strategic Assessment Element (SAE)	Our Firm's Position	Partner 1	Partner 2	Partner 3
Our Objectives				
Their Objectives				
Our Roles				
Their Roles				
Our Overall Resources				
Their Overall Resources				
Boundaries				
Market Model				
Strategic Exclusivity				
Intersections				

NOTES: Based on the results of step 3 (strategic fit assessment), fill out each cell in the "partner" column of the matrix with one of six symbols:

Symbol Meaning

OK   The partner accepts our position on the SAE.

?   We have a disagreement and are unsure of the resolution.

▲   We have a disagreement, but the partner is likely to accept our position.

•   We have a disagreement, but the partner's position is acceptable to us.

≈   A compromise can probably be negotiated that meets both firms' strategic needs.

x   A probable deal-killer. We have a disagreement and cannot accept the partner's position. An acceptable compromise is unlikely.

a biotechnology firm. The alliance will add the biotechnology firm's nutritional ingredients to the pet food company's existing product lines. The pet food company will distribute the improved products through its distribution network.

The pet food company began step 3 with two biotechnology firms on its short list, Company A and Company B. Both firms had genetically engineered nutrients to improve animal health. Following step 3, strategic fit assessment, it was clear that both companies had SAE conflicts with the pet food company.

Company A Conflicts. During the development of the Market Model in step 2, the pet food company's team specified that only the pet food company's brand would appear on the product. This requirement was also specified in the Our Objectives element. Here are the statements created for both of these Strategic Assessment Elements:

Our Objectives

"The pet food firm will establish and maintain its reputation for innovation through sole branding of any jointly developed product."

Market Model

"The customer will see the pet food company brand, not the biotechnology company's brand, on the product."

During the step 3 strategic fit assessment, it became clear that biotechnology Company A wanted its name associated with the new pet food. Company A's Market Model element stated:

Market Model

"Any jointly developed product will be cobranded."

During strategic fit discussions, Company A stated that it did not plan to compete with the pet food company. However, it did plan to sell nonfood products to pet owners. A cobranded pet food would introduce Company A's brand to pet owners in a powerful way.

Company B Conflicts. The conflict with Company B revolved around exclusivity. The pet food company's intent was to use this alliance to achieve a long-lasting advantage over its competitors. The pet food firm's Strategic Exclusivity element specified that:

> "The pet food firm will have global, perpetual, and sole rights to use the partner's novel nutrients in pet food."

Biotechnology Company B had a different view. While it was willing to give the pet food firm a one-year head start in the marketplace, Company B's strategic intent was to maximize the value of its ingredients by providing them to all pet food companies. Company B's Strategic Exclusivity element stated:

> "Company B will give the pet food firm a one-year exclusive right to use the nutrient, after which Company B will be free to provide licenses to others."

Figure 6-2 shows the Strategic Fit Reconciliation Map for this proposed alliance immediately following step 3. For simplicity, SAEs are omitted where both potential partners agreed with the pet food company's positions (i.e., an OK rating). The Strategic Fit Reconciliation Map includes brief statements of the pet food company's positions in each SAE; the potential partner's conflicting position is indicated in that partner's column.

Figure 6-2. Strategic Fit Reconciliation Map for pet food alliance after step 3.

SAE	Pet Food Company Position	Company A	Company B
Our Objectives	Sole brand	? (cobranded)	OK
Market Model	Sole brand	? (cobranded)	OK
Strategic Exclusivity	Exclusive rights	OK	? (one-year head start)

NOTES:
OK   The partner accepts our position on the SAE.
?   We have a disagreement and are unsure of the resolution.

Resolving the Disagreements. Faced with SAE disagreements, the pet food company Planning and Negotiating Team looped back to the Our Objectives statements of step 2 and other relevant elements. They challenged their original thinking with the new information. Is sole branding necessary? Can the pet food company label the products as "jointly developed with Company A" and still achieve its marketplace objective? Should the pet food company run the risk of establishing biotechnology Company A as the innovation leader in pet nutrition?

How about the disagreements with biotechnology Company B? Will a one-year head start allow the pet food firm to establish a strong enough foothold in the marketplace to fend off the competition? How will the pet food company deal with competing products using the same nutrient? Can the Strategic Exclusivity element be modified to meet Company B's concerns on market development by adding an "earned exclusivity" provision? That means the pet food company will remain the exclusive marketer of the nutrient as long as it sells a specified amount of pet food or pays agreed minimum royalties to the biotechnology firm.

During the loop-back process, the Planning and Negotiating Team reassessed its positions and considered where the partners might be flexible. The team concluded that the pet food firm could accept Company A's cobranding position, with specific treatment of how company brands would be displayed. However, Company B's one-year head start position on Strategic Exclusivity was not acceptable. Furthermore, the team concluded that a viable compromise was not possible, given Company B's clear strategy for widespread licensing.

The Strategic Fit Reconciliation Map was updated to reflect these new positions (see Figure 6-3) and documented in an updated version of the Alliance Framework document.

Figure 6-3. Strategic Fit Reconciliation Map for pet food alliance after loop-back through step 2.

SAE	Pet Food Company Position	Company A	Company B
Our Objectives	Sole brand	•	OK
Market Model	Sole brand	•	OK
Strategic Exclusivity	Exclusive rights	OK	X

NOTES:
OK   The partner accepts our position on the SAE.
•   We have a disagreement, but the partner's position is acceptable to us.
x   A probable deal-killer. We have a disagreement and cannot accept the partner's position. An acceptable compromise is unlikely.

The Resource Fit Reconciliation Map

The Resource Fit Reconciliation Map provides the same "one glance" summary of the resource fit that we just saw with strategic fit. Placing all key resources needed from the partner along the vertical axis and the list of potential partners along the horizontal axis, the Planning and Negotiating Team plots the results of the Tirekicks in terms of the quality and quantity of partner resources.

Figure 6-4 is the Resource Fit Reconciliation Map prepared by the pet food company team, based on Tirekick results. Both firms had outstanding research capability, and both could provide satisfactory technical support to the pet food company as new products were introduced to the market. Company B's ability to work closely with the pet food firm's staff to convert research results to marketable products appeared to be somewhat better than that of Company A.

Both Reconciliation Maps and the updated Alliance Framework with the team's conclusions were distributed to all stakeholders for comments. Stakeholder reactions confirmed that the pet food company could resolve its SAE conflicts with biotechnology Company A by agreeing to a cobranding arrangement in the Market Model. Though biotechnology Company B's resources were slightly better, their exclusivity position was a deal-killer. Based on the updated Alliance Framework, the pet food firm selected Company A for step 6 negotiations.

In addition to strategic and resource fit, there are other factors to consider when making the final decision. One is the level of motivation or self-selection that the potential partner has already made. Another is whether to choose one partner or multiple partners.

Figure 6-4. Resource Fit Reconciliation Map for pet food alliance after Tirekicks.

Key Resource	Company A	Company B
Ability to contribute to joint development of products based on preexisting nutrients	OK	OK+
Ability to provide technical support for jointly developed products	OK	OK
Ability to develop future nutrients	OK+	OK+

NOTES:

Symbol   Meaning

OK+   The partner's resources are outstanding and complementary to ours.

OK   The partner's resources are satisfactory and complementary to ours.

?   The partner has a weakness, but can overcome that weakness by adding additional resources.

▲   The partner has a weakness, but our combined resources can overcome the weakness.

★   The partner has a weakness that can be overcome through the use of third-party resources in a financially viable manner.

x   A probable deal-killer. The partner has a weakness that cannot be overcome through adding its own resources, using our combined resources, or with third-party resources.

Self-Selection: The Intangible Factor in Partner Selection

Strategic fit and resource fit are only part of the story. Vital motivation behind a successful alliance comes from the hearts and minds of key people. The question can be summed up succinctly: How committed are the management and staff of each potential partner to achieving the alliance's objectives? Remember the Battelle MicroCATS alliance? Battelle was not just interested in strategic and resource fits. The Battelle team members were seeking one or more partners as excited about MicroCATS technology as they were. That assessment can only be made by engaging the partner's people, understanding their motivations, and sensing their personal commitment to the project. When a firm's people have self-selected themselves into the deal, the energy that comes from self-motivation is tangible and translates into positive alliance results.

Self-motivation is critical to success. How did you assess the self-motivation of the partner in your last alliance?

The Multiple Partners Option

In the best case, one potential partner stands out above the others and is the clear choice for step 6 negotiations. Sometimes the strategic fit, resource fit, and commitment level assessments show that two or more candidates are highly qualified. In that case, the best course of action is to move forward to step 6 negotiations with multiple firms. Final partner selection is dependent on the results of other Alliance Framework elements, such as Financial Pie-Split.

There is another situation where multiple step 6 negotiations are required. Sometimes steps 2, 3, and 4 show that the alliance should be a multiparty relationship. For example, in Battelle's MicroCATS alliance, the resource fit assessments showed that an alliance with several partners could best meet Battelle's needs. If you decide on an alliance with multiple partners, before starting step 6 negotiations you will need to review the strategy fit and resource fit assessments carefully. In that review, you must evaluate the likelihood that all of the companies involved will agree to compatible positions on all Alliance Framework elements in step 6.

Tips for Completing Step 5 of the Alliance Framework

- Use the Strategic Fit Reconciliation Map and Resource Fit Reconciliation Map to compare the results of steps 3 and 4 among potential partners.
- Include a motivation assessment as a partner selection criterion.
- Loop back to step 2 with internal stakeholders to reassess your positions in light of new information.
- Select the best partner or partners for moving ahead to step 6.
- Look back at strategic fit and resource fit assessments for possible interpartner conflicts before attempting a multiparty alliance in step 6.

CHAPTER 7

NEGOTIATING THE AGREEMENT

The topic of negotiations has been discussed for centuries. Ever since the first cavemen bartered food for tools, people have debated the best way to strike a deal. There are many good books on the general aspects of negotiating techniques, and we won't review them here. Rather, we will discuss the aspects of negotiations that are especially important in alliances.

During steps 3, 4, and 5 of the Alliance Framework process, our company selected the most promising alliance partner (or partners) from the initial short list. The goal of step 6 is to get to a final agreement quickly, or find out fast that there are irreconcilable differences. During step 5, we picked our partner based on strategic fit and resource fit assessments in steps 3 and 4. In step 6, both firms use the Alliance Framework to plan and describe their positions on all elements of the alliance, to negotiate mutually acceptable positions where there are differences, and to record those negotiated positions in a format that can be readily converted into a contract. The two firms also use the Alliance Framework to jointly generate elements such as Detailed Objectives and Detailed Resources, which are cooperatively developed with each other.

We'll start with an overview of step 6, and then cover the details.

Negotiating a Common Vision of the Alliance

Just as the Alliance Framework enables stakeholders to reach internal consensus, it also enables both partner firms to negotiate a common "vision" of the alliance as it takes shape. By using the same set of elements with agreed-on definitions for each element, the firms minimize the opportunities for "I didn't know you meant that" misunderstandings later on. By working on all of the elements in parallel, the firms reveal the connections among the elements, disclose intent, and move the negotiations along quickly to a completed deal or a friendly walk-away.

Up to this point, the potential partners have devoted their attention to the Strategic Assessment Elements (SAEs). In step 6, they must negotiate the rest of the Alliance Framework elements. The first step is to identify those elements and clearly define each one. If the selected partner refuses to agree to a set of defined elements, that may indicate that you picked the wrong partner. It signals that your firm and the partner cannot agree on the central issues in your prospective alliance, even before attempting to agree on issue positions. For example, suppose the partner agrees to the inclusion of an Intellectual Property (IP) element in the negotiations, but does not agree that the Intellectual Property element should include provisions covering the use of IP following termination of the agreement. You have told the partner that the alliance may have a limited term, and you think that there must be a clear understanding on the post-termination rights to use intellectual property that will be commingled during the alliance. The partner objects, accusing you of planning for failure and arguing that post-termination provisions indicate a lack of trust. Either your firm is dealing with a partner with little experience in alliances and an unwillingness to learn, or one with a hidden termination agenda.

When firms do not agree on the definition of Alliance Framework elements, they may encounter the "I didn't know you meant that" problem during negotiations.
Have you ever run into that problem? What was the impact?

This example does not mean that the partner must take your firm's proposed elements and element definitions "as is." The partner may have important suggestions to make that your firm should be willing to negotiate. But an inability to come to agreement early in step 6 on relevant elements, and definitions of each of those elements, suggests that a deal-killer lies ahead. Agreeing on Alliance Framework elements and their definitions is fundamental to successful alliance negotiations.

The Use of the Alliance Framework Process in Negotiations

During the negotiation process, the firms compare their positions on commonly defined Alliance Framework elements and attempt to resolve the differences. All elements are discussed in parallel. Just as in the internal process, the two firms start by laying out their positions on every element. At the beginning of step 6, some elements other than the SAEs will be incomplete or even blank. The firms should not allow any element to be deferred. Early in step 6, both firms will work on their positions on every element and bring them to the table. For practical reasons, a specific meeting may concentrate on a few elements. Each meeting should include a brief status review of every element and a discussion of the schedule for progress on all elements. The intent is to work on the elements in parallel as the two firms attempt to move closer together in their positions on each element. Let's look at why parallel treatment is important.

Parallel Treatment of Elements During the Negotiation Process

Chapter 1 pointed out that the Alliance Framework document provides a complete picture of the intent of the alliance. Elements are designed to cover all important business aspects, and the deliberate overlap among elements helps ensure that stakeholders get a clear understanding of the ties to strategy and the prospective responsibilities of each internal organization. Those characteristics also apply to step 6 negotiations. By addressing elements in parallel, both firms quickly develop a common picture of the alliance or find that a common picture is not possible. Treating all elements in parallel reveals differences in strategic intent that may have been overlooked in step 3, strategic fit assessment.

Revealing Strategic Intent

The parallel treatment of elements encourages openness at the negotiating table. For example, consider an alliance between a U.S.-based manufacturer and a European-based competitor. The U.S. firm recently started a European marketing operation with limited resources. Those limited resources are inadequate to handle one important product line, which requires significant hands-on customer support. The European competitor has skilled marketing resources in place, but lacks the technology for the relevant product line. This could be a marriage made in heaven. The two firms conceive a straightforward alliance in which the products are designed and manufactured by the U.S. firm and marketed and supported by the European company. The SAEs in step 3 seemed well aligned; steps 4 and 5 went smoothly; and the two firms started step 6 final negotiations.

The two companies started working on all the remaining Alliance Framework elements in parallel. For example, negotiations began on the Financial Pie-Split, covering the transfer pricing of manufactured products and compensation for the European firm's sales efforts. The firms also started to develop Detailed Objectives, covering such matters as revenue projections and identifying the first target European customers for the product line. But the firms found that they had drastically different positions on the Term and Termination element and the Intellectual Property element. The European company wanted a long-term commitment, with significant constraints on either side's rights to end the relationship. It wanted to stipulate that a withdrawal by the U.S. firm would require a technology license from the U.S. firm, enabling the European firm to design and manufacture the product line.

The U.S. firm wanted a right to withdraw on short notice, with a commitment to satisfy existing orders, not future orders. As the two firms discussed their differences, it became clear that they had quite different pictures of the alliance in spite of the perceived SAE alignment in step 3. For the U.S. firm, the alliance was the best way to market the product line in Europe; however, the firm's managers thought that additional European marketing resources might be available at some later time. The U.S. firm wanted the flexibility to terminate the alliance and market the product itself in the future. The European firm had been working on the relevant technology, but it had not yet fully developed the technology or a product line based on the technology. In forming this alliance, the European firm's managers saw an opportunity to redirect limited R&D resources to other projects while offering the product line to customers. Because they would drop their R&D effort, the Europeans needed an assurance that their U.S. partner would not terminate the alliance and leave them with nothing to sell to their established customer base.

When the Planning and Negotiating Teams discovered that the two firms had major disagreements in the Term and Termination and Intellectual Property elements, their inability to quickly resolve the differences naturally led to the disclosure of each firm's intent. Given their positions on the two elements, it was difficult for either firm to hide their intents. The resulting frank discussion enabled the teams to develop a mutually acceptable resolution. They agreed on a time period during which the U.S. firm would not withdraw, and on Financial Pie-Split provisions to compensate the European firm if its U.S. partner decided to market the products in Europe in the future. Furthermore, the teams agreed on technology licensing provisions that would apply if the U.S. firm decided to market the products after the European firm's sales reached specific threshold levels. A clear understanding of each firm's intent allowed the teams to quickly reconcile their positions on all of the elements and move to a final contract.

What do we learn from this example? Parallel processing encourages early disclosure of intents and enables disagreements to be resolved through work on the overlapping elements affected by those intents. Parallel processing also minimizes the "Oh, by the way" problem that arises when elements are negotiated in series. In our European marketing example, the Planning and Negotiating Teams had much work to do on elements such as Financial Pie-Split and Detailed Resources. Suppose they had deferred work on the Term and Termination and Intellectual Property elements until work on the other elements was complete? Not only would much of that work have to be redone, but the "Oh, by the way" problem would have created serious distrust between the firms.

Notice that the disagreement exposed in the example was a possible "deal-killer." A deal-killer is an element that must contain certain provisions demanded by one side or else that side will not enter into the alliance—no matter how attractive the alliance looks in all other elements. The Term and Termination element (along with the related Intellectual Property element) had a potential deal-killer for both sides. Parallel treatment enabled the deal-killer to be exposed early and resolved.

Parallel treatment has another speed-to-deal benefit. Some elements (such as Detailed Objectives) often require considerable effort among marketing and other functional members of both teams. Those tasks can be assigned to specific Planning and Negotiating Team members of both firms and worked offline while other elements are being negotiated. In that way, important but lengthy cooperative work will not delay reaching a final agreement.

The Step 6 Process Sequence

The core events of step 6 are a series of interfirm meetings in which the Planning and Negotiating Teams present positions on each Alliance Framework element and attempt to resolve differences. Early in these meetings, remaining SAE issues and likely disagreements in all other elements are identified. The two teams discuss each element in order to reach mutually acceptable resolutions. Sometimes element disagreements are resolved during the meeting, but often both teams need the opportunity to reflect on their positions after the meeting. Between meetings, each team develops its ideas on how element disagreements might be resolved and revises its firm's internal Alliance Framework document based on the interfirm discussions and those team ideas. The revised Alliance Framework document is the tool for ensuring stakeholder understanding of interfirm disagreements, and for receiving stakeholder input for dealing with them. By keeping a regularly updated Alliance

Framework in front of stakeholders during negotiations and receiving continued stakeholder input, the Planning and Negotiating Team keeps the internal alliance together as the external alliance takes shape. Stakeholder disagreements on interfirm issues are aired and settled through the firm's normal management decision process. This regular updating avoids a deadly pitfall—having the deal that's negotiated at the table depart from the deal as initially understood by internal stakeholders. That common problem results in an "I never knew that was in the deal" attitude among key stakeholders and sets the stage for implementation failure.

During negotiations, the terms of the alliance may evolve from the initial understanding of internal stakeholders. What process does your firm currently use to keep stakeholders apprised of the changes?

During Step 6, both teams remain alert to the emergence of an unresolvable deal-killer. Just as in preceding steps, both must be conscious of the need to terminate the discussions and part friends if that happens.

As the two Planning and Negotiating Teams' positions move closer and closer together, the teams start working on a mutual Alliance Framework document that reflects the developing element agreements. That mutual document, after all element disagreements are resolved, is the starting point for contract drafting by both firms' legal counsel.

The Dynamics of the Negotiating Process

How should the Planning and Negotiating Teams exchange information and positions between meetings? How should meeting notes be recorded and shared between the firms? Should Team Leaders interact one-on-one to resolve sticky points? The answers to these and other negotiating questions depend on factors such as the experience of both teams, the complexity of the alliance, cultural and language gaps between the firms, and management preferences. Good judgment on the best choices come with experience, but there are a few common aspects of negotiation dynamics, such as negotiation meeting styles and deal fever, that are important to understand.

Negotiating Meeting Styles

Team members new to negotiations often have questions about style. Should the team have only one person speak at the meetings, or can everyone participate freely (as in internal meetings)? Should the team use the "good cop, bad cop" method, in which one person takes a hard line that is then softened by others?

One principle is that the Team Leader must be the person who expresses the positions of the company's top management. That doesn't mean that the Team Leader must do all the talking during negotiating sessions. On the contrary, designated team members may describe the team's positions on a specific Alliance Framework element and lead the discussion with the partner on that element. However, the Team Leader must remain clearly in charge. That can be done by offering judicious summations of the company's positions on important points, by calling on others to speak, by calling for a caucus, or by suggesting to the other firm that there is a need for post-session reflection or additional work on a sticky disagreement.

The Planning and Negotiating Team's positions on each element must be agreed upon in advance. The negotiating table is no place for brainstorming, and it's an inappropriate place to blurt out positions not previously considered by the team. As positions are explained and intents revealed, possible solutions to disagreements become apparent. Depending on the nature of the problem and prior consideration of that problem by internal stakeholders, the team may suggest a solution to the other side after a team caucus. In a caucus, the team will discuss the solution in private and may contact internal stakeholders by phone. Alternatively, the possible solution may require looping back to stakeholders after the meeting, with resolution in a follow-up communication with the partner.

We are skeptical about the "good cop, bad cop" negotiating style. First, it is usually a transparent ploy. More important, it raises doubts about the quality of the firm's internal alliances and the thoughtfulness of the firm's positions. Our advice: Don't use it.

Deal Fever

Deal fever is a syndrome that affects many alliance managers. The symptoms are a need to sign the deal regardless of newly revealed strategic disagreements or other adverse events that happen at the negotiating table. In a very real way, the deal takes on a life of its own. Team members have invested significant time as well as physical and emotional energy into the alliance. They unconsciously protect the deal from collapse, even when it becomes apparent that the alliance should not happen. When deal fever infects top management, it is even more damaging. Top managers sweep away every obstacle to getting to a final agreement. Internal critics are silenced. Well-thought-out stakeholder objections to proposed changes in the firm's earlier element positions are given short shrift. Deal-killers are ignored. The deal is going to happen, regardless of the ultimate consequences.

Has your firm ever signed a deal because someone in your company had deal fever? Did an executive on the other side have deal fever? What were the consequences?

What is the cure for deal fever? There is no magic elixir. However, the use of the Alliance Framework can help treat the disease. Since the firm carefully plans and documents its element positions in step 2, proposed element changes based on interfirm negotiations force the Planning and Negotiating Team and all other stakeholders, including top management, to examine the effects of possible negotiated changes. If a position on the Intellectual Property element demanded by the partner flies in the face of your firm's Our Objectives statement, why go ahead with the deal? Even with the help of the Alliance Framework tool, the only sure cure for deal fever is experienced and competent management who will walk away from a bad deal.

Why Win-Win Is More Than a Buzzword

How important is the concept of "win-win" in alliance negotiations? Crucial. If the Planning and Negotiating Team is clever enough to negotiate a win-lose alliance, they'll often kill the deal. Unhappy partners stop executing. They deploy high-quality resources to profitable programs and send the leftovers to the alliance. Management focuses attention on why a bad deal was signed, not on how to maximize the value of the alliance.

Just what is "win-win," other than a general idea that both partners gain from an alliance? Equity Theory helps with a better definition to guide negotiations. Equity Theory states that the ratio of each party's inputs to outputs in any exchange should be one. A firm bringing 20 percent of the inputs to an alliance should receive 20 percent of alliance outputs. A partner bringing 80 percent of the inputs should receive 80 percent of the outputs. Equity Theory goes beyond that simple ideal formula, adding the insight that each person's motivation and contributions to the alliance will depend on the individual's perception of the actual ratio. The smaller the perceived ratio of outputs received to inputs contributed, the less each person is willing to contribute to the alliance. Let's explore the implications for alliance implementation.

Humans are little computing machines. We constantly calculate our contribution to the organization and compare it to two reference points: our reward/contribution ratio and the reward/contribution ratio of others. Examples abound in the area of employee compensation. When the organization rewards everyone at the same rate regardless of individual contributions, high performers are motivated to do less. Policies or union contracts that require everyone to receive an identical raise tend to demotivate high performers. Similarly, team-based reward systems that provide every team member with the same reward overcompensate the slackers and undercompensate major contributors. Equity Theory argues that when the reward/contribution ratio is out of whack, with 80 percent of inputs rewarded with 20 percent of outputs, people have only two choices: Either increase their rewards or decrease their contribution. Since the rewards are outside the person's control, the only option is to decrease contributions. That is the behavior we see in the workplace.

How does this theory apply to alliances? Partners who feel that they have entered a "win-lose" deal stop executing. They go through the motions but contribute little else. People point fingers, looking for reasons and scapegoats for the unfavorable deal. Contractual provisions tied to performance only fuel the fire as people try to prove the other side stopped executing. The seeds of alliance implementation success and failure are planted in the negotiations of the contract. Negotiating a "win-lose" alliance is a recipe for implementation failure.

Tips for Negotiating During Step 6 of the Alliance Framework

- Agree on relevant elements and their definitions.
- Negotiate all elements in parallel.
- Keep internal alliances healthy through updating the Alliance Framework document and circulating it to stakeholders.
- Be alert for unresolvable deal-killers.

- Prepare a mutually agreed-on Alliance Framework document as the starting point for the alliance contract.
- Avoid deal fever.
- Avoid "win-lose" alliances.

CHAPTER 8

ALLIANCE FRAMEWORK ELEMENTS OTHER THAN THE STRATEGIC ASSESSMENT ELEMENTS

After years of using the Alliance Framework in various industries, we find that a similar list of elements can be used to create a complete business picture of any prospective relationship. Why? Ninety percent of the issues in every alliance are identical. How firms resolve those issues varies widely and depends on the specific alliance in question. However, the issues themselves transcend industries, companies, and international borders. Similarities of Alliance Framework elements follow directly from similarity of issues. For example, every alliance is based on objectives of the parties, which must be complementary if the alliance is to succeed. Every alliance requires the partners to agree on the resources each will bring. Every alliance must include a clear understanding of the rights of each partner to use the intellectual property of the other that is disclosed in the course of cooperative work.

Therefore, the Planning and Negotiating Team can develop an element list and definitions for any alliance by starting with the typical list and fine-tuning it to fit the specific situation. The remainder of this chapter is a detailed discussion of each element on the typical list, beyond the Strategic Assessment Elements (SAEs). The intent of the chapter is to clearly define each element and describe common pitfalls Planning and Negotiating Teams encounter as they develop their positions on each element.

Adding Elements Not on the Typical List

The typical list of Alliance Framework elements is now familiar (see Figure 8-1). For a specific alliance, the Planning and Negotiating Team should start with the typical list and add elements to fit its unique circumstances. New elements may be required by special aspects of the alliance or by a team decision to highlight certain issues. Pharmaceutical alliances contain a Regulatory element to clearly expose each firm's view of the Food and Drug

Administration (FDA) issues related to the alliance. Internet alliances contain a Privacy element to ensure both firms agree on the collection and use of individual data.

What elements are unique to your industry or to your prospective alliance as you create an Alliance Framework element list?

Figure 8-1. Typical list of Alliance Framework elements.

```
Business Plan Summary
Objectives
    1. Ours
    2. Theirs
Roles
    1. Ours
    2. Theirs
Overall Resources
    1. Ours
    2. Theirs
Boundaries
Market Model
Strategic Exclusivity
Intersections
Detailed Objectives
Detailed Resources
Financial Pie-Split
Intellectual Property
Working Process and Governance
Term and Termination
```

"Boilerplate" in the Alliance Framework

In any alliance contract, legal counsel for both sides draft mutually acceptable provisions intended to deal with commonly encountered contractual rights and obligations of the partners. Some examples are waivers, representations and warranties, notice requirements, force majeure statements, and choice of law provisions. Business people sometimes refer to these contractual statements as "legal boilerplate." Some business people ignore these statements because they think they are unimportant and believe their counsel will protect the firm's interests. This can be a mistake. Any of these provisions in an alliance contract can be crucial under certain conditions, and each must be thoughtfully understood, planned, and negotiated.

Should any of these provisions be included in the Alliance Framework process, addressed either as part of a typical element or included as a separate element? Sometimes, yes. For example, a dispute resolution provision is often included in the Working Process and Governance element. A choice of law provision should be included in an Alliance Framework between two firms from countries with different legal systems, such as an alliance between a U.S. and Japanese firm. In some alliances, indemnification for patent infringement is important. The Planning and Negotiating Team must consider whether other common contractual provisions have enough potential impact on the alliance to require coverage in the Alliance Framework. The judgment call is this: Are the parties likely to have different points of view on a significant issue? If so, the issue should get the attention of both teams in step 6 (negotiating an agreement) by being included in an Alliance Framework element. The trade-off is between neglecting an important issue in the Alliance Framework and diverting team attention to routine matters. The lawyer on the team should advise on that trade-off.

The Detailed Objectives and Detailed Resources Elements

A quick glance at Figure 8-1 shows that the words Objectives and Resources appear twice on the list of typical elements. The first time they appear as the SAEs Our Objectives, Their Objectives, Our Overall Resources, and Their Overall Resources. The second time they appear is in step 6, where they are spelled out in far more detail. Consider an alliance between a consumer marketing company and an engineering firm, aimed at developing a new power toothbrush. Do the firms agree that the alliance should develop a new battery-powered toothbrush to sell for $10, with market launch within two years? That question should be covered in the elements Our Objectives and Their Objectives. Do both parties understand that the engineering firm will supply all the mechanical and electrical engineering expertise, and the marketing partner will supply all the required marketing insights and skills? That question should be addressed in the elements Our Overall Resources and Their Overall Resources. These elements, along with the other SAEs, help the partners assess strategic fit.

Once the firms agree they are strategically aligned, they must go beyond those SAEs and develop detailed positions on the related elements: Detailed Objectives and Detailed Resources. These elements require the level of precision needed to begin alliance implementation. For example, what are the mileposts in the design, manufacture, and launch of the new $10 toothbrush? What consumer tests will trigger a commitment to full-scale manufacture, and what evaluation criteria are appropriate? What engineers and marketing people will each firm commit to the project? What are the engineering and marketing budgets?

Firms encounter a number of challenges as they develop these two elements. Chief among them is the differing skill sets each firm brings to the alliance. In the toothbrush example, an engineering firm is the technology source and the marketing firm is the market-facing partner. While each is skilled in its own area of expertise, it is unskilled in the partner's area. While that complementary fit can make a great alliance, it also complicates negotiation of the Detailed Objectives and Detailed Resources elements. The marketing firm may be clueless on engineering mileposts or what constitutes a reasonable engineering budget. The engineering firm may be equally uninformed on what consumer tests are required, or how long consumer testing should take. Even if both firms have enough knowledge (or try to fill knowledge gaps by hiring outside consultants) to make independent estimates of these two elements, the nature of these elements requires that they be developed cooperatively. That means the alliance negotiation, as applied to Detailed Objectives and Detailed Resources, is in large part a cooperative planning process.

This raises an obvious dilemma. How does each firm deal with the risks of cooperative detailed planning when the deal is not yet signed? Can each firm accept the disclosure risks that are required to cooperatively develop the Detailed Objectives and Detailed Resources elements, knowing that the deal may not happen? The answer is yes, because there are two risks that can be more damaging than overdisclosure.

The first is the "workability" risk. The only way prospective partners can accurately determine the workability of the alliance is by developing the Detailed Objectives and Detailed Resources elements. For example, while the firms may agree to design and market a low-cost power toothbrush in two years, the discipline of working out the details of timelines and budgets will provide significant insight into the reality of the shared objectives. Without joint effort on these two elements, the firms may enter into an alliance only to discover that the project is unworkable. Experience shows that the risk of operational failure is greatly reduced after these two elements are carefully developed through cooperative work between the partners.

The second risk is the "Day 1" problem. The scenario goes like this: Now that two firms have signed the alliance contract, hoisted the champagne glasses, and come to work the next day, what do they do? Without adequately defined Detailed Objectives and Detailed Resources elements, fledgling alliances spin their wheels for months while managers responsible for alliance implementation develop a work program, determine budgets, and shift resources from internal projects. Internal disagreements on resource allocations, which should have been identified and resolved before implementation began, emerge to cause mischief. Sometimes they are ultimately solvable, sometimes not. In any case, they should have been identified and resolved before the deal was signed, avoiding delay and frustration.

Developing these two elements requires a careful balancing of risks. Generally, prospective alliance partners err on the side of underemphasizing the importance of these two elements. This is due to a tendency to over-weight the disclosure risk and underweight the workability and Day 1 risks.

The following sections discuss the remaining Alliance Framework elements and identify common issues associated with each one. Let's start with the Financial Pie-Split element.

Financial Pie-Split Element

This element addresses the way in which financial rewards and risks are allocated between partners. Typically, the element contains one or more formulas that describe that allocation. An example of a formula is the royalty rate paid by the market-facing partner to the engineering partner bringing the underlying technology. The Financial Pie-Split element has an unlimited number of possible solutions because the financial circumstances of each alliance are unique. Therefore, there is no typical way to develop the structure of this element. While the details of alliance financial structures are beyond the scope of this book, we will outline some basic principles that should guide teams as they plan and negotiate this element.

The Financial Pie-Split element must include a financial model (or formula) that balances the preexisting and future values brought by each firm. Values can be such things as patents and technical know-how, skills such as engineering or marketing capability, marketplace position, or funding. The challenge for the Planning and Negotiating Teams is to define those values and convert them into a mutually agreeable formula (or formulas).

Many firms begin to construct the Financial Pie-Split element by estimating the financial metrics of the business opportunity created by the alliance. In the $10 power toothbrush example, the teams agree on projections of sales, costs, capital investment, and other financial metrics for the toothbrush. Using net present value (NPV) techniques, the financial projections are converted into formulas for royalties or other cash transfers between the partners.

In alliances where there are transfers of goods or services between the partners as part of alliance implementation, the financial aspects of these transfers must be included in the overall financial model. For example, suppose one partner manufactures and markets toothbrushes that incorporate power supplies made by the other partner. The transfer price of the power supplies is an explicit part of the alliance financial model.

The Planning and Negotiating Teams must agree on an important decision: Should the Financial Pie-Split element be a rule-based or transactional model? Let's define each and consider the implications:

● *Rule-Based Model.* The partners agree on a rule, or collection of rules, for the financial model. In the simplest case, the rule lasts for the term of the alliance. A fixed royalty rate is a classic example of a rule-based model: The marketing firm will pay the engineering firm a 4 percent royalty on sales of the toothbrush for the agreed term of the alliance. Rule-based models can be much more complex than this example to deal with future uncertainties. The basic idea is that the parties will build those uncertainties into the formulas at the time the alliance agreement is signed.

● *Transactional Model.* The partners agree that certain aspects of the financial terms will be subject to negotiated revision at specified times. For example, the teams can agree in step 6 that the transfer price of the toothbrush power supplies will be renegotiated every year.

What are the implications of choosing a rule-based or transactional model? Generally, rule-based models are more difficult to negotiate. While the fixed royalty example seems straightforward, in practice the negotiations can be complicated because the parties have to agree on possible future scenarios. What are the likely annual sales, and how should the royalty rate be adjusted if actual sales are higher or lower than initially projected? Could costs be higher or lower than estimated, and how should cost variations be built into the financial model? The challenge of designing a rule-based model is to reward both firms fairly in light of future uncertainties. Resolving that challenge can add considerable time to reaching a final agreement.

Transactional models are simpler to develop and negotiate. In the toothbrush power supply example, the partners agree that they will negotiate a new transfer price if the power supply costs more than expected at the end of the first year. However, a transactional model has one major drawback. What happens if the partners cannot agree on a new power supply transfer price at the end of the first year? That adds uncertainty to the alliance and acts as a source of conflict during implementation. Every time the transfer price is renegotiated, arguments arise as to expense allocations and other accounting issues. The energies devoted to negotiating the new transfer price just reallocate the rewards of the alliance between the partners, diverting management's attention from meeting customers' needs and dealing with the competition.

Like many other matters in the Alliance Framework, there is no right answer. The choice of a rule-based model or a transactional model depends on the characteristics of the specific alliance. But the Planning and Negotiating Teams must understand the trade-offs.

Finally, the financial rules must be straightforward enough to be managed by ordinary mortals during alliance implementation. A brilliantly conceived and negotiated financial model is worse than useless if managers on both sides struggle to make it work on a day-to-day basis. This unhappy event occurs when sophisticated financial managers develop a Financial Pie-Split model that deals with every possible outcome. Trouble arises when responsible implementers do not understand the model or find that required information is difficult or impossible to develop. While there is no hard-and-fast rule, Planning and Negotiating Teams should develop a simple model that people on both sides understand and can apply without wrangling during implementation.

Intellectual Property Element

The use and protection of intellectual property (IP) is poorly understood by many managers and team members. An otherwise healthy alliance can collapse because of the misuse of shared intellectual property. Sometimes the misuse is real because the offending partner deliberately violates a clear contract provision. In most cases, the misuse stems from a genuine misunderstanding about the intellectual property rules of the alliance.

It is impossible to describe the typical content of an

Intellectual Property element because the appropriate provisions are situation dependent. We can, however, describe general principles that should guide both teams' thinking.

The first step toward developing a set of workable intellectual property provisions is to define the types of IP relevant to the alliance. The obvious types are patents, proprietary technical know-how, trademarks, and copyrights. But any information or knowledge that enables one firm to distinguish itself from its competitors can be significant intellectual property. Examples may include customer lists, knowledge of customer preferences and willingness to pay, or the methods used by a consumer-products company to evaluate the marketplace attractiveness of a new product. All of these may be closely guarded trade secrets. To the extent this information is shared with an alliance partner, the allowed use of that information must be covered in the Intellectual Property element.

Developing Intellectual Property Positions

Developing the firm's positions on the Intellectual Property element requires close coordination between the business and legal members of the Planning and Negotiating Team. Why? The positions are tied directly to the business intents of the alliance. The lawyer must understand business intents, and the business people must understand how their intents will be met by the appropriate application of IP law.

Let's use a simple example to illustrate the tie between business intent and the Intellectual Property element. Suppose a large firm and a small firm intend to use certain preexisting technology of the small firm to cooperatively develop Product A. They agree that the product

Boundaries of the alliance will be Product A. However, the large firm also wants to use the small firm's preexisting technology outside the Boundaries to independently develop Product B. The large firm is willing to pay royalties to the small firm for that privilege. Part of the benefit that the large firm counts on from the alliance is that broader right to use the small firm's preexisting technology. This business intent should lead to a provision in the Intellectual Property element that gives the large firm specified rights to use the small firm's technology outside the Boundaries. As the outside Boundaries aspects of the Intellectual Property element are negotiated, the large firm's business intent for Product B will be clearly revealed.

That tie between business intent and element provisions has important implications not only for the Intellectual Property element but also for the entire Alliance Framework process. Notice that the large firm's business intent for Product B was revealed through its position on the outside Boundaries provision in the Intellectual Property element. That intent could not be hidden. If both firms understand all of their business intents, all Alliance Framework elements can be negotiated smoothly and naturally. The firms can get to a mutually acceptable deal or part friends, quickly.

Ownership vs. Rights-to-Use Intellectual Property

Business managers and their legal counsel often focus on the concept of "ownership" when negotiating intellectual property rights. Each side attempts to retain, or gain, ownership of intellectual property. The underlying thought is that ownership gives the owner clear rights to intellectual property and allows the owner to deny those rights to anyone else, including the partner. This tactic often leads to prolonged arguments at the negotiation table and poorly defined intellectual property rules.

In our experience, an initial focus on ownership is misdirected. Rather than ownership, business people should first deal with "rights to use" (RTU) intellectual property, under specified circumstances and terms. Rights to use means exactly what it says. The firm has a right to use specified intellectual property as defined in the agreement. Those RTU are directly connected to the marketplace. Initial focus on RTU enables the firms to negotiate a set of intellectual property positions that reflect each firm's business intent, independent of who owns the intellectual property.

A straightforward application of this principle is the large firm's use of the small firm's preexisting technology to develop Product B. In this example, the large firm does not need to "own" the small firm's technology. However, the large firm must have a specified right to use that technology for Product B, where "use" can mean the manufacture and sale of products based on the technology, or the right to sublicense the technology to others. Through an understanding of the large firm's business intent and the disclosure of those intents to the small firm, the required RTU are developed in the Intellectual Property element of the Alliance Framework.

Our emphasis on RTU does not suggest that ownership is unimportant. Quite the contrary. Depending on the legal system governing the alliance, ownership can have important implications for such matters as patent infringement actions. However, the initial team focus in planning and negotiating the Intellectual Property element should be on RTU. The partners should first develop appropriate RTU rules starting from the business intents of both. If mutually agreeable RTU rules can be negotiated, counsel for both sides can then translate those rules into ownership provisions that conform to applicable legal requirements.

The Six Dimensions of Intellectual Property

Teams should develop RTU rules for each relevant type of intellectual property across six dimensions:

- *Background and Foreground.* These two dimensions describe when the intellectual property was developed. Preexisting intellectual property brought into the alliance by one partner is called "background." Intellectual property developed during the course of the alliance is called "foreground."
- *Inside and Outside.* Will the intellectual property be used inside and/or outside the Boundaries of the alliance?
- *During and After.* Will the intellectual property be used during and/or after the term of the alliance?

Figure 8-2 illustrates these six RTU dimensions in a matrix, with typical examples of types of intellectual property along the horizontal axis. By developing a set of RTU rules that cover the relevant cells of Figure 8-2, alliance partners convert their business intents into a set of RTU rules to govern the alliance.

The shaded cells in Figure 8-2 illustrate a commonly encountered IP issue in the conversion of business intents to RTU rules. During the term of an alliance, each partner will normally have certain rights to use the background patents of the other, within the Boundaries of the alliance. For example, a partner manufacturing and marketing a cooperatively developed product (i.e., a product within the Boundaries) based on the other firm's preexisting (i.e., background) patents must have rights to use those patents while the alliance is in place. But what happens after the alliance is over and the partners are no longer involved in ongoing cooperative work? Will the manufacturing and marketing partner retain any right to use those patents, perhaps with certain limitations and with an ongoing royalty obligation to the other firm? Agreeing on an answer depends on whether there is agreement on the partners' intents for independent marketplace participation after the alliance ends. The firm providing the background patents may be reluctant to see its former development, manufacturing, and marketing partner in the marketplace after the cooperative work of the alliance has ended. On the other hand, the manufacturing and marketing partner may view its continued marketplace participation with the developed product as vital to its business strategy. Those intents must be clearly understood by both firms and discussed during step 6 negotiations. If the partners can negotiate mutually acceptable intents for the post-alliance marketplace, the relevant RTU rules can be readily developed.

Each aspect of business intent can be described by using an RTU submatrix, as shown in Figure 8-3 for the Product A/Product B example. The large firm wants to use the small firm's technology in Product B. That means that the large firm needs the right to use the small firm's background technology (as well as the foreground technology from the alliance) for applications outside the Boundaries, during and after the term of the alliance.

Figure 8-2. Typical rights-to-use matrix: one issue highlighted.

	Patents	Technical Know-How	Marketing Information	Business Practices
Background	(highlighted)			
Foreground				
Inside Boundaries	(highlighted)			
Outside Boundaries				
During Alliance				
After Alliance	(highlighted)			

Detailed RTU rules are developed that apply to the cells in Figure 8-3. Some details are:

- What specific patents and technical know-how does the large firm require?
- Will the outside Boundaries RTU be limited to Product B, or to a larger group of potential products outside the Boundaries?
- Will the RTU be granted to the large firm in an exclusive arrangement?
- Will the RTU be limited in specified ways, such as rights to sublicense or within geographical limitations?
- What will be the financial terms of the license?

By filling in the RTU rules for the cells in Figure 8-3, the intellectual property provisions of the alliance are connected to the large firm's business intent for Product B. That connection makes RTU the most effective initial focus in developing the Intellectual Property element.

Disclosure

Disclosure is another concept in the Intellectual Property element. It refers to the extent to which specific intellectual property of one partner must be revealed to the other. Disclosure rules are tied to both implementation aspects of the alliance and to broader business intent. Again, we'll use the Product A/ Product B situation as an example.
It is not necessary for the small firm to disclose substantial portions of its background technology to the large firm if the large firm does not need that technology to

Figure 8-3. Rights-to-use submatrix for Product B.

	Patents	Technical Know-How
Background		
Foreground		
Outside Boundaries		
During Alliance		
After Alliance		

carry out its alliance Roles for Product A. If, on the other hand, the firms agree that the large firm will have the right to use the small firm's background technology for Product B (outside the Boundaries), then there must be a corresponding, more extensive disclosure requirement. The large firm's outside Boundaries RTU is useless if the small firm does not disclose enough of its background technology to enable the large firm to develop Product B independently of the small firm.

Confidentiality

Confidentiality refers to the conditions under which the partners may reveal specific intellectual property to third parties. There are often legitimate needs to disclose proprietary IP to others during implementation. An example is the situation where the market-facing partner enters into contractual relationships with third parties to provide technical support to customers. In that case, the third-party technical support team may require background and foreground technical information to support customers. To develop confidentiality provisions, the Planning and Negotiating Teams must discuss likely implementation scenarios and agree on appropriate confidentiality rules to fit those scenarios.

The Embedding Problem

The embedding problem refers to the situation in which one firm becomes so polluted with the other's intellectual property that it cannot help but use it. Intellectual property is both "leaky" and "sticky." Once two firms work together, intellectual property leaks from one to the other. Once someone learns the intellectual property of the other firm, it sticks with them and is used for a variety of purposes. Consider an alliance in which a U.S.-based manufacturer of machine tools allies with a Taiwanese partner to jointly develop a new line of tools and to manufacture those tools in the Taiwanese firm's factory. In order to achieve cost objectives, the U.S. firm plans to provide its proprietary manufacturing control software to the Taiwanese partner. The Taiwanese partner points out that its factory makes machine tools for other firms on a contract basis, including competitors of the U.S. firm. It is impossible for the Taiwanese firm to use the manufacturing control software only for manufacturing products developed in the alliance. Once the software is integrated into the operations of the factory, the United States firm's background technology is embedded in the Taiwanese firm's operations. It cannot be extracted.

Here's a different embedding example. Suppose a market-facing partner agrees to share foreground marketing information it develops during the alliance with its technology partner. However, the market-facing partner insists that the technology firm use that foreground information only for the purposes of the alliance and only during the term of the alliance. What happens to the business prospects of the technology firm if the alliance ends? With these restrictions, the technology firm might be barred from that market. Since the technology firm cannot use the data, it has to independently re-create the marketing information. That re-creation is difficult to do because the technology firm's employees are contaminated with the data from the partner.

What's the solution? During the planning and negotiation of the Intellectual Property element, the teams must identify where embedding may lead to conflict. Some embedding is unavoidable but harmless. Some potentially harmful embedding is avoidable by simply agreeing not to transfer certain intellectual property between the partners. The situation that requires careful attention is embedding that is unavoidable and potentially damaging to one or both parties under some conditions such as termination of the alliance. Each embedding possibility must be addressed and a solution found during step 6, final negotiations.

Have you learned something from your partner that is embedded in your organization? Was that situation anticipated in the alliance contract?

The solutions are varied and situation dependent. In our machine tool example, the U.S.-based firm must weigh the advantages and disadvantages of providing its software to the Taiwanese partner. Perhaps the United States firm will agree to grant a royalty-bearing license for all uses. But perhaps not—in which case the partners will agree to implement the alliance without the benefit of the software. In our foreground marketing information example, the partners might agree to allow the technology firm to use the data, or they may agree that certain data will be withheld from the technology firm to avoid contamination. The crucial need in both cases is for the Planning and Negotiating Teams to identify each potential embedding problem and resolve them during step 6.

The "Joint vs. Sole" Question

This question is important in any technology development alliance, whether the development effort is large or small, breakthrough or ordinary. No matter the circumstances, the "joint vs. sole" question must be answered.

Here's how the question arises:

Let's look at an alliance between Company A and Company B, which involves the cooperative development of new technology. The Roles element in the Alliance Framework for the alliance assigns development tasks to each firm. Some tasks are assigned specifically to one firm, while other tasks are to be carried out jointly. Regardless of the task assignments, the quality of the results depends on effective communication between the scientists and engineers of Company A and those of Company B. Through both formal means, such as regularly scheduled meetings and exchange of memoranda, and informal means, such as phone calls and one-on-one visits to each other's laboratories, technical people from Company A and Company B communicate results, exchange ideas, and critique each other's work. During those interactions, new ideas are generated that may lead to important patents or provide the foundations for new proprietary technical know-how.

Now let's consider the joint vs. sole question. The IP element in the Alliance Framework includes RTU rules for foreground technology (i.e., technology developed in the course of the work in the alliance). For example, there will be rules for the rights to use foreground patents outside the Boundaries of the alliance. The joint vs. sole question as applied to this example is: Shall Company A's and Company B's rights to use foreground patents outside the Boundaries be independent of whose people came up with the patentable idea? Or, shall those rights depend on which partner's technical people made the patentable invention?

In the former case, where Company A's and Company B's rights to use will not depend on the source of the invention, we refer to a "joint" approach to RTU rules. In a joint approach, the partners have agreed to ignore the source of an idea for RTU purposes. Even if a scientist from Company A makes a patentable invention entirely on her own, Company A's and Company B's rights to use that patent outside the Boundaries will be the same as if the invention were made by a scientist from Company B. From an RTU perspective, the partners have agreed that all patentable ideas will be treated as though they were jointly conceived between Company A and Company B.

In the latter case, where the rights to use will be different, depending on which company conceived the idea, we refer to a "sole" approach to RTU rules. Where the scientist from Company A conceived the patentable idea "solely" (i.e., without someone from Company B), then Company A's rights to use that patent outside the Boundaries will be different (typically more favorable to Company A) than if the idea had been conceived by a scientist from Company B. In a "sole" approach, the firms' rights to use are independent of the source of the idea only in those situations where people in both Company A and Company B actually jointly conceived the idea.

While we have discussed the joint vs. sole question in terms of RTU foreground patents outside the Boundaries, the same question is applied to other dimensions, such as rights to use technical know-how after the term of the alliance.

Let's first look at the consequences of the joint

approach to RTU rules. When firms choose the joint approach, they agree to ignore who came up with the invention for RTU purposes. While patent law requires identification of the inventor for a patentable invention, the RTU objectives of this approach can be achieved through appropriate licensing provisions in the alliance contract. In a joint approach, the two firms' scientists and engineers will be open with each other because it doesn't matter whose firm makes an invention or develops know-how. The formal and informal communications essential to success will go well because of this openness. But there is a downside. For example, if both firms have equivalent rights to use, there can be severe conflict in the market-place. In one worst-case scenario, the noninventing firm can license an invention to a competitor of the inventing firm, regardless of the inventing firm's objections.

Now let's look at the implications of a "sole" answer to the question. When the alliance agreement uses a sole approach, both firms will be vitally interested in keeping track of whose scientist or engineer came up with each new idea, since each firm's RTU will be impacted by the source of the idea. For example, the RTU rules might be that each partner will be able to exploit its own sole fore-ground inventions for all purposes, while the noninvent-ing partner has very limited RTU. That would have little impact inside the Boundaries during the term of the alliance because the RTU foreground inventions will be clearly specified in the Roles element. But inside the Boundaries after the term of the alliance, or outside the Boundaries during or after the term, each firm may be going its separate way in the marketplace. With strict lim-itations on the noninventing partner's rights to use, each firm will be confident that its own inventions will be safe from exploitation by the partner outside the agreed Roles in the alliance. So far, so good. There is a downside, though. In the sole approach, the partners place a barrier in the path of collaborative work. During the collaboration, both firms' technical staffs will be conscious of who came up with what idea. Discussions will be guarded at best, stifled at worst. Lawyers from both sides will be regularly involved to carefully note who originated each idea. The impact is chilling to technology exchanges and restricts the free flow of ideas that leads to innovation.

How has your firm dealt with the "joint vs. sole" question in technology alliances?

There is no single right answer to the joint vs. sole question, and the best answer in a specific alliance involves a thoughtful judgment call. Teams should consider how closely the firms' technical staffs will work together, as well as the consequences of worst-case scenarios on both firms' marketplace intent. For example, where the technical collaboration requires close day-to-day work between partners, the chilling effect of the sole approach can be lethal to implementation. To the extent that technical tasks are well separated, then the chilling effect becomes less crucial because innovation is less dependent on scientists and engineers from the two firms interacting closely together. When the marketplace implications of granting significant RTU to the noninventing partner are onerous, the sole approach may be best.

Working Process and Governance Element

To ensure smooth implementation, the partners must plan and negotiate the methods through which the partners will work together. At the simplest level, this Alliance Framework element addresses the management processes that the partners use to implement the alliance. It includes such matters as the organization of interpartner committees and working groups, how the partners will share information, and the creation of top executive steering committees that will review contentious issues that threaten the health of the alliance. It also details the methods partners will use to communicate, monitor progress, and deal with daily concerns.

At a deeper level, it specifies which partner will make each type of major decision and whether those decisions will be consensual or the responsibility of one partner. Anyone who has worked in an alliance where all major decisions are made by consensus knows the problem. When one firm is clearly an expert in a particular area and the other is not, consensual decision making slows the parties down and wastes resources. Time, effort. and emotional energy are frittered away as the expert partner justifies its position to the nonexpert partner. When both firms are experts or neither is an expert, consensual decision making leads to higher-quality decisions and commitment to carry out the decision. Our bias is to strike a balance in decision-making styles. When one firm is clearly an expert in the area, that firm makes the major decisions with input from the partner. When both firms, or neither firm, are experts, consensual decision making is preferred.

When negotiating this element, Planning and Negotiating Teams work with legal counsel to agree on the legal methodology to resolve disputes that cannot be handled through top management discussions. For example, should the parties move to arbitration prior to a lawsuit? Should the arbitration be binding or nonbinding? How is the arbitrator chosen? The answers to these questions depend on the preferences of both firms, the subject matter of the alliance, and (in the case of cross-border deals) the applicable legal systems.

Term and Termination Element

In general, alliances do not last forever. Every alliance agreement (and every Alliance Framework that provides the substance for drafting the agreement) must specify the circumstances and impacts of potential termination. The Term and Termination element not only spells out those separation terms, but also provides essential insights into the business intents of both partners.

Why are alliances terminated? The most common reasons are:

● The objectives of the alliance were successfully achieved, and the partners want to proceed in the marketplace independently.

● One of the partners changed its strategic direction or decided that other projects have a higher priority.

● One of the firms has identified a better partner and wants to form a new alliance with that partner.

● One or both partners decided that the implementation results are less successful than initially expected and that future prospects are not encouraging.

● One partner has not performed adequately or has breached the terms of the alliance contract.

● One partner was acquired or merged with another company.

In negotiating the Term and Termination element, legal counsel for both partners must be involved in discussions on how these possible reasons will be addressed in the alliance agreement. For example, how inadequate performance is handled and what constitutes a "breach" have business and legal implications that depend on alliance circumstances. There are, nonetheless, some general principles that Planning and Negotiating Teams should recognize.

One such principle is the idea that both partners should have a right to withdraw from the alliance under specified circumstances. That does not imply that a partner can simply pick up the marbles (i.e., the values it brought into the alliance or the fruits of the alliance work) at any time and go off on its own. But it does mean that an unhappy partner should not be forced, by the conditions of the alliance agreement, to keep performing indefinitely. Such provisions make no practical sense. The unhappy partner will go through the motions, but its best resources will be devoted to other projects.

In planning and negotiating the Term and Termination element, the teams should address issues such as:

● Shall the alliance have a fixed term, or should it go on forever until one partner or the other decides to terminate it?

- Under what circumstances should a partner have a right to withdraw? Shall a partner have the right to withdraw for "no reason" (i.e., without having to justify its withdrawal decision based on specific criteria)? Or should the partners have to use an objective criterion such as a failure to meet a milepost? Or should the withdrawal criteria change over time (i.e., where the partners are more tightly bound to the deal for some limited time, after which withdrawal is easier)?

- Shall the RTU residuals—that is, the assets of the alliance that remain after termination (e.g., foreground intellectual property)—depend on which partner withdraws and the circumstances of that withdrawal? Or should the RTU residuals be independent of the identity of the withdrawing partner (the equivalent of a "no-fault" divorce)?

- What phase-down rules should be implemented to govern the ways in which the alliance activities will wind down? This is particularly important in market-facing alliances where matters such as continuity of supply to customers and ongoing customer support must be assured.

In some situations, the overall intent of the Term and Termination element may be to allow each partner to proceed in the marketplace without the other. But that's not always true. One partner bringing critical background intellectual property into the alliance may be reluctant to allow the other partner to proceed independently with that background intellectual property if the other partner decides to withdraw. Or a firm that expects to contribute important foreground technology during a development program may be unwilling to allow a withdrawing partner to carry that foreground technology away.

Resolution of these matters requires open discussion of both partners' long-range intentions during step 6. As we pointed out earlier, each partner's intentions are revealed by the positions taken on all Alliance Framework elements. That is especially true in the Term and Termination element. To use a crude example, suppose my position on the Term and Termination element is that my firm should be able to terminate the alliance for no reason on ninety-days notice, and that I should be able to proceed independently in the marketplace using all of your background intellectual property and all foreground intellectual property. With such a position, you might be a little suspicious about my intent. While this outrageous example makes the point, the Term and Termination element always forces the parties to reveal their intentions. That's why this element, like all Alliance Framework elements, must be part of the step 6 parallel process described in Chapter 7.

Alliance Structure Element

This final Alliance Framework element describes the structural aspects of the relationship. Should the partners be bound by a contractual agreement between the two firms? Should the firms establish a new joint venture entity? Should a joint venture rely on the parents for required resources such as professional skills or develop the needed skills in-house? Do one or both firms plan a spin-off to execute the alliance strategy?

In most cases it is best to treat these issues after the

other Alliance Framework elements are reasonably far along in step 6. The most appropriate structure will be evident after the partners make progress on the Detailed Resources and the Financial Pie-Split. But there are some situations where the Alliance Structure element should be covered earlier. A large pharmaceutical firm was planning an alliance with a small technology start-up to develop and market a new medical device. Since that product was outside the mainstream of the large pharmaceutical firm's business, the firm wanted to establish the alliance as a separate joint venture with the start-up. To focus attention on this intent, the pharmaceutical firm included Alliance Structure as an SAE in step 3 discussions. Alliance Structure might be an up-front matter in some international alliances as well, where local laws or customs require a joint venture structure.

In most cases, however, the most appropriate structure will suggest itself to the partners during step 6 negotiations. We do not recommend beginning the process with a specific structure in mind and trying to force the Alliance Framework to fit that structure. It's better to begin the process by taking the business opportunity through the Alliance Framework technique and letting the structure present itself.

Tips for Alliance Framework Elements Other Than the SAEs

- Agree on relevant elements and their definitions early in the discussions.
- Start with the typical element list and add elements to fit the specific alliance.

- Carefully evaluate which "boilerplate" matters are important enough to be addressed in an Alliance Framework element.
- Work cooperatively to thoroughly develop the Detailed Objectives and Detailed Resources elements.
- Ensure that the Working Process and Governance element anticipates how the partners will work together during implementation.
- Focus first on RTU in the Intellectual Property element, then ask the lawyers to translate these rules into the appropriate ownership provisions.
- Use the negotiations of the provisions of each element, such as Term and Termination, to reveal strategic intents.
- Defer, whenever possible, making your decision on the Alliance Structure element until progress is made on the other elements.

PART 2

IMPLEMENTING THE ALLIANCE

CHAPTER 9

THE ALLIANCE IMPLEMENTATION PROGRAM

Being a mariner in the year 600 A.D. was a risky business. Swift currents, rocky shoals, and constantly shifting sandbars conspired to ruin experienced and inexperienced sailors alike. Most captains stayed within sight of land. Only the bravest ventured past the horizon into the unknown. With the introduction of the navigation chart, everything changed. Captains knew with certainty what lay ahead. They could plan, predict, and prepare. It's true that plenty could still go wrong, and it often did. But the value of having a clear vision of the path forward was immeasurable.

Alliance managers venture into the unknown every day. Few have a navigation chart that pinpoints the rocky shoals of integrating skill sets or predicts the swift currents of linking decision-making structures. Fewer still have a clear vision of how the shifting sands of corporate culture impact the ongoing relationship. The purpose of the Alliance Implementation Program (AIP) is to provide managers in both companies with a navigation chart they can use to plan and execute the implementation phase of the alliance.

Eli Lilly and Company: An Example of Alliance Management

In 1924 Eli Lilly scientists were desperate to strike a blow at diabetes. They believed that by joining forces with researchers at the University of Toronto they could develop the first injectable insulin. That project was one of the great medical challenges of its day, and for diabetic patients with no medical alternatives, the stakes were high. This strategic alliance was the first of many that positioned Eli Lilly as a leader in diabetes care.

By the 1980s, diabetes was controllable, but far from beaten. The swine insulin of the day caused allergic reactions in some patients, violated the religious principles of others, and was often in short supply. Because insulin was derived from the pancreas of pigs, it was subject to the vagaries of the pork market. When pork supplies were high, insulin was abundant and relatively inexpensive. When pork supplies were low, supplies of insulin were low and relatively expensive. Eli Lilly scientists knew that the power of biotechnology could produce another breakthrough: unlimited amounts of pure human insulin. To turn their vision into reality, Lilly formed a relationship with Genentech, Inc. Together they revolutionized the process of insulin production by using *E. coli* bacteria as miniature factories to produce unlimited amounts of pure human insulin.

Eli Lilly executives did not stop there. They collaborated with Takeda Chemical Industries, Ltd. of Japan to sell Takeda's oral antidiabetic medicine through Lilly's marketing organization. They joined forces with Alkermes, Inc. to cooperatively develop an inhaled form of insulin. If that effort is successful, diabetic patients will be able to throw away their needles and dose themselves with a refreshing deep breath. In 2002, Lilly formed an alliance with Amylin Pharmaceuticals, Inc. to develop and market Amylin's diabetes drug AC2993. The hope is that the drug will lower the level of fructosamine, a kind of sugar, in patients with Type 2 diabetes. This problem affects 90 percent of the 17 million diabetics in the United States.

Alliances are a central tool for carrying out Eli Lilly's strategy. Senior executives are dedicated to making Lilly the most sought-after partner in the pharmaceutical industry. They are building alliance management capabilities throughout the company, developing state-of-the-art alliance processes and systems, clearly articulating corporate policies related to alliances, and tying employee compensation packages to the success of the alliances under their care. Lilly's goal is to earn the title "Pharmaceutical Partner of Choice" by maximizing, continually improving, and over-delivering on every one of hundreds of alliances. You can be sure that the company's extensive alliance portfolio includes a set of relationships that will propel it to a position of leadership in the next generation of diabetes treatment.

Eli Lilly and Company has taken alliance navigation to new heights.[1] The company's Alliance Database contains details on hundreds of alliances. Its Office of Alliance Management has scores of people dedicated to improving the performance of every alliance. Lilly surveys each of the firm's alliance partners annually, asking detailed questions on how Lilly is perceived as a partner. The bottom-line questions are: "How are we doing?" and "What can we do better?" Lilly's extensive alliance network justifies the resources and the organizational commitment to such a comprehensive program. However, most companies need something different: a simple, low-cost program that is easy to use but very powerful. They require a program that provides alliance managers with the tools they need, when they need them, in an easy-to-use format. The Alliance Implementation Program is designed to be exactly that.

The AIP tools rose from the ashes of many failed alliances. After we visited dozens of sick alliances, some themes began to emerge. Good managers in great companies fell into the same traps. The Alliance Implementation Program identifies those traps and provides managers in both alliance partners with the tools they need to navigate their way to success.

Although these tools were initially developed to turn around sick alliances, the worst time to use them is when the patient is ready to expire. The Alliance Implementation Program should be used to help alliance Operating Managers build healthy alliances on day one. When the day-to-day operation managers from both firms come together and link decision-making structures, coordinate resource allocations, employ conflict management techniques, and develop meaningful trust measures, they successfully navigate through some of the most treacherous waters in alliance management.

To describe the use of the AIP tools, we will begin by describing a typical interfirm coordination structure and the roles of key people in alliance implementation.

The Implementation Team

Because the scope of alliances and the size and management structure of firms vary so widely, the specific membership of the Implementation Team must be tailored to the situation. But there is an overall approach that works well. At the beginning of alliance implementation, top management of both partners should identify a specific group of people who will be responsible for coordinating the resources of both firms. Most of these people represent stakeholder organizations assigned to carry out implementation tasks. While they often have significant tasks to perform themselves or through organizations that they personally manage, their responsibility goes beyond those tasks. As part of a larger stakeholder organization, they must ensure that promised resources are applied to tasks and that alliance problems are exposed and resolved. For example, a large company responsible for an alliance global marketing function might appoint a marketing group leader from its European office to represent the entire worldwide marketing function. This person's coordinating job goes beyond Europe. He or she will deal with alliance marketing issues worldwide, working closely with counterparts in North America and Asia. This job requires the ability to influence peers and to escalate issues when required. Top management must find the right balance, selecting the right people to handle these coordination tasks so that there is appropriate coverage without creating an Implementation Team that is too large to be effective.

In this book we will refer to this group of people as the Implementation Team. Their job is fundamentally different from the Planning and Negotiation Team. At this point the alliance exists, and both Implementation

Teams must make sure that the alliance achieves its goals and objectives. As pointed out in Chapter 1, continuity of key people between the planning and negotiation steps and implementation is essential. One good way to do this is to assign people from the Planning and Negotiation Team to the Implementation Team.

AIP Variability Among Firms and Alliances

The specific ways that the Alliance Implementation Program is carried out will vary depending on the size and organizational complexity of both firms and the scope of the alliance. The roles described in this chapter for managers and individual contributors may be partitioned in many ways. In large company/small company relationships, the small firm may have one person performing several implementation roles while the large company partner may have one person dedicated to each role. We gave an example earlier where a single European manager represents a global marketing organization of a large firm. That structure might not work in some companies, and several marketing people may be on the Implementation Team. In a small firm or in an alliance with a narrow scope, the Implementation Team might include all the people with alliance tasks.

The Alliance Implementation Program has been adapted for use in many situations, and readers should consider how that adaptation might best be done in their particular alliance. Now, let's turn our attention to a typical Implementation Team.

Alliance Executive

The Alliance Executive is the top executive responsible for alliance success. The Alliance Executive may have the profit-and-loss responsibility for the business unit most affected by the alliance, or could be the senior functional executive at the center of the alliance's purpose. For example, in an alliance involving the joint development of a new product or service, the Alliance Executive might be the head of the relevant strategic business unit (SBU). In a global marketing alliance, the Alliance Executive could be the worldwide head of marketing and sales. This person should be able to allocate resources needed by the alliance or work with other senior executives on resource issues. The Alliance Executive speaks for the firm in the event of serious alliance disagreements with the partner. The Alliance Executive has oversight of the firm's Implementation Team.

Alliance Operating Manager

The Implementation Team is led by an alliance Operating Manager who, working with the partner's Operating Manager, has the day-to-day responsibility for coordinating and integrating the activities of the two firms. This role will generally be a major part of the assigned person's job and may be a full-time assignment. In this role, the Operating Manager reports to the Alliance Executive.

CHARACTERISTICS OF THE ALLIANCE OPERATING MANAGER

While planning for the creation of a multiparty alliance, a client asked this insightful question: What are the characteristics of a successful alliance Operating Manager? Four characteristics are key to success in this role. First, the Operating Manager must be competent in the focus area of the alliance or must have the background to become competent quickly. In an R&D relationship, this means understanding the technology at a deep enough level to predict the probability of overcoming hurdles and knowing how much time any particular task should take. In a marketing relationship, it means understanding the customer at a deep enough level to predict the effects of pricing strategies and evaluating the implications of market research. The importance of this competence goes far beyond the need for this person to understand the activities of the alliance. Team members look up to managers who are experienced professionals as well as strong leaders.

This person must also be a competent project manager. At their core, alliances are massive project management exercises. The tools, metrics, and management techniques of project management provide structure and direction to the task of coordinating the resources of two firms. They allow managers to integrate the skills of various groups inside each firm and between the partners. Project management is a well-understood and mature science. Selecting someone who understands this science is a source of advantage for the alliance.

The Operating Manager must be well respected and understand the political structure of the manager's own firm. Alliances require the hand of a savvy politician. Internally, the person must be able to gain access to resources through the informal network. The manager must have the respect of key decision makers in all stakeholder organizations and be seen as a future leader of the firm. Externally, the Operating Manager must protect the partner. The Operating Manager must be able to argue the partner's case, deflect attempts to re-deploy alliance resources, and defend the partner against the organization's immune system that seeks to attack anything "not invented here." People newly hired into the firm as alliance Operating Managers often stumble. They lack the organizational experience that forms the basis of power.

The final characteristic is the most difficult to describe. The Operating Manager must be an "old soul," someone who has lived many lifetimes. A person who is mature in personality and can comfortably engage others will move the alliance along in unseen ways. The best way to describe this characteristic is to describe its opposite. Some people dig in their heels on every little matter and fight to the death. They are aggressive, assertive, and combative. Compromise is a word they don't understand, and every loss is recorded as a basis for future revenge. These people can destroy an alliance. Better to select an Operating Manager who understands the art of compromise. Look for people who pick their battles carefully and can win while allowing every other combatant to win a little something as well. While you can teach people project management techniques and they can acquire technical competence, the skills of an "old soul" are a gift, and one that is crucial to the alliance's success.

Implementation Team Members

One or several members of the Implementation Team may represent each stakeholder organization. They may have significant line management responsibilities or may be individual contributors to the alliance. But to be effective, an Implementation Team member must have "informal power" inside the stakeholder organization. That means the person must have the ear of stakeholder management and the ability to drive resolution of alliance issues inside the stakeholder organization.

Alliance Support Specialist

The alliance Support Specialist is a person trained in the use of alliance management tools and in providing implementation support to one or more alliances. Companies vary widely in the existence of these people and in assigning their responsibilities. Eli Lilly and Company's extensively trained specialists are assigned to each Implementation Team. Often, firms do not assign specific individuals to this role and the support tasks are carried out by the Operating Manager. Since support in applying the tools of the Alliance Implementation Program (outlined in the next section) is critical to effective implementation, both firms should ensure that a specific person is assigned to this role and provided with the proper training.

Integrating the Alliance Implementation Program Into the Normal Workflow

Alliance Operating Managers and Support Specialists take great care to integrate their activities into the normal workflow of each company. Powerful interventions can only be made at specific points in time based on how ready the workforce is to accept the new alliance. The same interventions attempted at other times can negatively affect performance. The best alliance support programs have a goal of providing greater than 50 percent improvement in performance while using less than 3 percent of the team member's time. One way to achieve this goal is to leverage current in-house tools and processes. For example, sophisticated management infrastructures such as project management, Six Sigma, and quality initiatives guide behavior in the organizations that employ them. The likelihood of acceptance and effectiveness is increased by integrating alliance tools and management techniques into existing workflow. The following twelve tools of the Alliance Implementation Program will help you do that.

The Twelve Tools

1. Joint Negotiator Presentation
2. Intellectual Property Disclosure Rules
3. Implementation Plan Workshops
4. Stakeholder Mapping
5. Decision-Making Analysis
6. Expectation Mapping
7. Conflict Prediction

8. Breakdown Sessions

9. Trust Self-Assessment

10. Technology Transfer Questions

11. Arguing the Partner's Position

12. Valuing the Partner's Contribution

The first six tools help the Operating Manager overcome organizational boundaries that doom alliances. They are covered in this chapter. The next six tools help managers deal with conflict. These tools are covered in Chapter 10.

The first use of the tools should be at the join-up session.

Join-Up Sessions

The join-up session is the first meeting between all of the members of both Implementation Teams. In part, a join-up session is a celebratory kickoff meeting where Implementation Team members get to know one another and begin the process of collaboration. There should be plenary sessions, workshops, and recreational events.

The specific purposes of the join-up session are to:

- Ensure that all members of both teams clearly understand the letter and spirit of the alliance agreement.

- Introduce both teams to tools, metrics, and management techniques that Operating Managers will use to facilitate implementation.

- Enable the teams to jointly develop the Implementation Plan, including deliverables and metrics.

- Build the interpersonal relationships important to alliance success.
- Begin the collaborative process outlined in the Implementation Plan.

The Six Tools to Overcome Organizational Boundaries

The first six tools are used to help the Implementation Team cross organizational boundaries. It is best to use each of these tools at the initial stages of implementation and reuse each as appropriate during quarterly meetings. The first step is to come to agreement with the partner on which tools are appropriate for the current alliance. Not all firms are comfortable with all six tools. Some large firms have their own tools that integrate into the corporate infrastructure. Many small firms have none. In either case, both Operating Managers must come to agreement on the value of the tools and how each will be used in the alliance.

Tool 1: Joint Negotiator Presentation

Transferring the language of the alliance contract into easily understood concepts and communicating those concepts to Implementation Team members is a major stumbling block in alliances. Failed alliances often share a common characteristic: People from both firms misunderstand important aspects of the contract on the very first day.

This situation is guaranteed to occur when Implementation Team members learn about the alliance in the usual way. A supervisor describes his or her best understanding of the alliance to each person on the Implementation Team. Most people get it about 80 percent right. Implementation Team members fill in the remaining 20 percent with well-intentioned "Scientific Wild Ass Guesses" (SWAGS) that quickly take on the aura of fact. Worse yet, the partner's Implementation Team learns about the alliance in the same way. They also get it 80 percent right; but it's a different 80 percent. They fill in the blanks with their own hopes and desires . . . and the alliance spirals out of control from the very start.

Alliances do not stand a chance when Implementation Team members from both companies misunderstand the contract on day one—and don't know it.

The Joint Negotiator Presentation deals with this common pathology. During the first plenary session the negotiators from both companies give a joint presentation describing every aspect of the alliance contract. To prepare for that meeting, some companies ask each Implementation Team member to read the jointly developed Alliance Framework or the alliance contract prior to the session.

The presentation works best when the negotiators start with a clearly articulated vision of the alliance and statements of intent from both parties. It continues with a complete description of the agreed-on positions on each Alliance Framework element (see Chapter 8, Figure 8-1). Most important, the presentation does not end until every team member's questions have been answered. Tool 2, Intellectual Property Disclosure Rules, is a key part of this discussion.

Tool 2: Intellectual Property Disclosure Rules

Team members must have a clear and unambiguous understanding of the intellectual property provisions of the contract. As discussed in Chapter 8, intellectual property includes patents, trademarks, and technical know-how, as well as any other information that enables a firm to distinguish itself from its competitors. Implementation Team members must understand all of the intellectual property rules of the alliance, as described in the Alliance Framework and written in the alliance contract. Every aspect that affects day-to-day interactions, such as the resolution of the "joint vs. sole" question, must be clearly understood by all members of both teams.

The alliance contract provisions that govern disclosure of trade secrets are especially important in day-to-day alliance implementation, which is why the Alliance Implementation Program focuses on Intellectual Property Disclosure Rules as a distinct tool. The best method of communicating these disclosure rules is for the alliance Operating Managers to first take their Implementation Team aside and clearly describe each concept in Figure 9-1. Then the partners can ensure a common understanding of the disclosure rules during the join-up session.

Each Implementation Team member must understand what intellectual assets of the firm are relevant to this alliance. Next, they must have a clear understanding of which intellectual assets, held as trade secrets, must be disclosed to the partner, under what circumstances and in

Figure 9-1. Intellectual Property Disclosure Rules.

What trade secrets of our firm are relevant to this alliance? For example:

- Potentially patentable inventions prior to patent issuance
- Proprietary chemical formulations
- Manufacturing process details
- Materials specifications
- Product design methodology
- Testing procedures
- Software source code
- Business practices
- Customer lists
- Results of marketing surveys

According to the alliance agreement, identify which of the above-listed trade secrets:

__ Must be shared with the partner and at what level of detail
__ May be shared with the partner and at what level of detail
__ Must never be shared with the partner

what detail. For example, the partners in a joint development alliance where work is allocated between the partners' laboratories will usually agree on full bilateral disclosure of laboratory results. Depending on the nature of the alliance, certain trade secrets may also be disclosed even though there is no specific contractual requirement to do so. An example might be the disclosure of an efficient testing process to enable one partner to better evaluate materials supplied by the other.

Absent a common understanding of the intellectual property rules, Implementation Team members from both sides are reluctant to share the trade secrets of their firm. This reluctance is misinterpreted as noncooperation or worse. The resulting confusion escalates quickly as each side sees the other as uncooperative. What is the solution? A clear and common understanding, developed at the join-up session.

A different kind of havoc arises if a partner provides information that was intended to be held back, because rights-to-use (RTU) rules are often connected to specific assumptions about what trade secrets will not be disclosed.

Let's look at an example in an alliance that includes a marketing and sales aspect. Assume that the market-facing firm has agreed to disclose its overall marketplace insights, such as general customer preferences, to the partner. However, the market-facing partner has not agreed to disclose customer-specific information, such as sales, prices, and other sensitive information to the partner. With those disclosure rules, the market-facing firm granted the partner broad rights to use disclosed marketing information, both inside and outside the Boundaries of the alliance. These RTU were agreed upon as the way of dealing with the embedding problem discussed in Chapter 8.

Now suppose an Implementation Team member of the market-facing firm, in the spirit of alliance cooperation, provides customer-specific information to the partner. According to the contract, the partner is free to use that information, both inside and outside the Boundaries. Additionally, the partner may believe that since the customer-specific information was volunteered, the ethics of the situation allow free use. This situation creates an opportunity for anger on both sides, which can poison the atmosphere and provide additional opportunities for attorney's fees.

Understand what information you must and must not share. Loose lips sink partnerships.

Tool 3: The Implementation Plan Workshops

Since the primary output of the join-up session is the Implementation Plan, much of the effort will be devoted to developing specific strategies for assets and business processes that directly affect the success of the alliance. Each agreed-on aspect of the Implementation Plan will have objectives and timetables to set the stage for day-to-day action and follow-up review at subsequent meetings.

The Implementation Plan is developed through focused workshops involving selected members of the Implementation Team. The number of parallel workshops and the focus of each workshop are tailored to the specifics of the alliance. A global alliance involving cooperative R&D, joint marketing, and shared manufacturing operations will have parallel workshops covering each area of cooperation, with agendas tailored to the most important anticipated issues.

The jointly negotiated Alliance Framework and the alliance contract are the basis for the Implementation Plan. For example, the Detailed Objectives element in the Alliance Framework will describe specifications and timetables for the first jointly developed product in an alliance. However, for work to move forward effectively, far more operational detail must be developed. The preparation of the Implementation Plan requires team members from both partners to discuss the operational aspects of the alliance in an intensive way, beginning with a common understanding of all Alliance Framework elements. Since the firms are now allied, all necessary details can be openly shared. In that way, the Implementation Plan fills gaps in the Alliance Framework, drives each Alliance Framework element to greater specificity, and enables the fast start of day-to-day cooperative work.

The workshop structures and agendas are strongly influenced by the focus of the alliance. The following is an example:

Workshop 1: Products/Services/Markets

- Market positions of each company, including a review of customers and competitors
- Market opportunities for the products/services covered by the alliance
- Obstacles and issues such as customer reactions, overlaps, and conflicts
- Product/service portfolio to be developed and marketed
- Processes for cooperative product/service design and realization (e.g., design methodology, gates, testing)

- Detailed roles for each partner in product/service development
- Detailed objectives for first jointly developed product

Workshop 2: Customer Relationships

- Roles in customer interfaces (e.g., sales, customer support, invoicing)
- Marketing communications (i.e., how the alliance is positioned with customers)
- Processes for identifying and soliciting new business
- Configurations, quotes, pricing, order entry, follow-up
- Sales forecasting and measurement systems
- Customer support (e.g., technical assistance, warranties)
- Physical distribution processes

Workshop 3: Intra-Alliance Operations

- Alliance governance
- Intra-alliance product/service transfer processes
- Day-to-day working processes
- Conflict resolution
- Compatibility issues such as manufacturing processes, quality, financial reporting, information technology
- Personnel assignments and policies
- Formal and informal information transfer
- Budgeting, cost allocation, revenue sharing

The results are captured in a working document that is the raw material for the final Implementation Plan. Members of each workshop present their results to the Implementation Teams of both partners for discussion. Modifications are made to the conclusions and timetables. Task group assignments are made to deal with unresolved issues. The result is a detailed, agreed-on Implementation Plan focused on each area of cooperation. The Stakeholder Mapping and Decision-Making Analysis tools allow team members to further sharpen the focus of the Implementation Plan.

Tool 4: Stakeholder Mapping

Coordinating and integrating the resources of two firms is a fundamental challenge to every alliance. Alliances rarely have resources of their own. Rather, they rely on stakeholders in both firms to provide the quantity and quality of resources needed to accomplish alliance goals. This places the alliance in competition for resources with the internal projects portfolio of each firm, and that competition is ruthless. Using a thousand forms of treachery, internal project managers beg, borrow, and steal the best resources of the firm to maximize the performance of their project. Alliance managers must fight for their fair share.

The Stakeholder Mapping tool (see Figure 9-2) guides alliance managers as they compete for resources. It is best used at the functional level to determine how firms will meet the resource needs of the marketing or the manufacturing function. For this reason, this tool works well when used in the Implementation Plan workshops. Beginning with the Alliance Framework and the alliance contract, each workshop specifies the sources of the resources needed to accomplish its goals. Using the Stakeholder Mapping tool, Operating Managers develop their strategy for acquiring the quantity and quality of resources needed from each firm to succeed.

Alliances populated by the dead wood of each partner, with access to the lowest-quality resources of each firm, never win the Baldrige Award.

Most of the columns and rows of the tool shown in Figure 9-2 are self-explanatory. However, there is value in reviewing the "buy-in strategy" column and the rows labeled "key people" and "keep informed."

Figure 9-2. Stakeholder Mapping.

	Name	Resources	Timing	Buy-In Strategy
Key People				
Keep Informed				
Wounded Princes*				

* Discussions of these people should take place only in one-to-one conversations between Operating Managers, for professional and legal reasons.

Stakeholder Buy-In. The stakeholder buy-in column asks a political question. How did the Operating Manager of the alliance convince the person who controls a specific resource to provide high-quality resources to the alliance? What does the stakeholder gain in return? Organizations are politically charged environments. Power, favors, and deference are the coin of the realm. Resources are the most visible form of power and are tightly controlled. The stakeholder buy-in column asks the difficult question: Why should the stakeholder give the alliance high-quality resources or any resources at all?

This column also addresses a common misery in alliances. Jointly the partners have 90 percent of the talents and resources needed for success, and each was expecting the other to bring the remaining 10 percent. This problem is avoided through a candid discussion of resource contributions in the context of accomplishing goals and milestones.

At this point the reader may ask why Stakeholder Mapping is needed at all, since stakeholder buy-in is an important objective of the Alliance Framework process. In an ideal world, all stakeholders in both firms will be ready to devote required resources at the conclusion of the Alliance Framework process. In the real world, it doesn't always work that way. Hence the need for Stakeholder Mapping.

Organizational Politics. The "keep informed" and "wounded princes" rows in Figure 9-2 further explore the impact of organization politics on the alliance. The "keep informed" row identifies people in each company who can influence the course of future events. These people are valued allies. By forming coalitions and avoiding conspiracies, Operating Managers shape the alliance.

Is there a moment in time when Stakeholder Mapping is particularly important? Yes, during the budget cycle. The budget is the best indicator of each partner's future intent. Since budgets are created twelve to eighteen months in advance of actual expenditures, each partner knows its intentions early on. The budget is an extremely effective early-warning system for identifying changes in each partner's resource commitments and strategy. As a general rule, each partner should have "look in rights" into the budget of the other as that budget relates to the alliance.

Politics and budgets are tightly linked. If you want to know your partner's future intentions, follow the money.

Wounded Princes. Not everyone is happy when an alliance is formed. There are winners and losers in both firms. Winners find their skills in high demand. Losers look at the partner and say to themselves, "Those people are doing my job, and they are doing it better than I can."

When people feel threatened, the normal human reaction is survival. The instinct is for people to defend their role, their department, and their system. People argue their case to re-create their credibility. This leads them to conduct themselves in a manner inconsistent with the goals of the alliance. Using a hundred forms of sabotage, they slow the alliance down, dissipate its energies, and deflect its momentum in unproductive ways. Sometimes the sabotage is blatant. Usually it is subtle, but the result is always the same. Dealing with wounded princes is an art form, and a delicate one at that. While no single solution exists, there are two strategies managers use to minimize their power: identification and co-optation.

Sunlight is the best disinfectant. Wounded princes are effective because they fly below the radar screen and cause trouble quietly. Once managers in both companies identify the wounded princes in their own firm, the princes' ability to do harm is minimized. It is difficult to cause trouble quietly when management is aware that a person's motives are not aligned with those of the alliance team.

Co-optation is another strategy. Co-optation is a big word for converting an enemy into a friend. This solution is effective when alliance management can create a value-added role for the wounded prince inside the alliance. Co-optation has been used for centuries in international relations, politics, and now alliances.

A word of warning: Although we have seen the Stakeholder Mapping tool (Figure 9-2) filled out numerous times, we have never seen the "wounded princes" line actually filled out, and we hope we never do. A discussion of wounded princes should take place in a one-on-one conversation between Operating Managers. The goal is to identify who may resist the alliance while protecting that person's reputation, dignity, and employment status. There also may be legal ramifications if the person is later terminated from the firm.

Tool 5: Decision-Making Analysis

Decision making is a fundamental aspect of every organization. Each partner has a decision-making structure that forms the basis of its processes and systems. For example, the decision-making structure determines how resources are allocated, priorities are set, and product introduction decisions are made.

The problem in alliances is that the partners' decision-making structures are usually incompatible. As one manager put it, "An alliance is like two boats, tied together, sailing through rough waters. When one captain turns, the other captain better know about it." Decision-making structures are the organizational equivalent of a rudder.

The idea that decision-making structures are incompatible is a concept that holds true in many types of alliances: large company/small company, United States/Japanese alliances, co-promotion deals, industry/university collaborations, and collaborative R&D agreements. This notion even holds true when two firms use the same generic decision-making structure, such as stage gates, because each firm adapts the stage gate process to fit its internal systems and structures.

The Decision-Making Analysis tool allows managers to understand each other's decision-making structure and jointly develop a strategy for making collaborative decisions in the alliance. Notice the column headings in Figure 9-3. In contrast to the popular notion that decisions are made in a structured and ordered way, the "informal process" column acknowledges the "garbage can model"[2] of organizational decision making. The garbage can model sees companies as loosely coupled collections of managers who use inconsistent and ill-defined preferences to make decisions. Organizations survive despite the fact that employees vary in the amount of time and effort they devote to a task. The company is a place where issues are looking for decisions, choices are looking for problems, and managers are looking for work. Sound familiar? The garbage can model encourages managers to think about the informal organization as a predictable source of resources that are tapped in self-seeking ways.

Figure 9-3. Decision-Making Analysis: How are decisions made in your company?

Upcoming Alliance Decisions	Key People	Formal Process	Informal Process	Time to Decision	Type of Information	Date Needed

The Decision-Making Analysis worksheet is best used during the Implementation Plan workshop sessions. Each workshop uses the tool to determine how decision making will impact the deliverables. The process begins by asking the Operating Managers to identify three to five key decisions they must jointly make during the next six months. Those decisions are listed along the vertical axis of Figure 9-3. Next, both managers identify the person in their company who has the authority to make those decisions, what formal process the firm uses (e.g., stage gate), what informal process is used (i.e., how the firm really makes decisions), and the time it takes to make a decision of that magnitude. The "time to a decision" column recognizes that some firms make decisions very quickly while others do not. Conflicts on timing usually lead to frustration as one firm waits for the other to decide.

Also in Figure 9-3, note the "type of information" and "date needed" columns. These represent another common information flow problem in alliances: disconnected corporate timetables. Some firms work on a calendar year, others are on a fiscal year. Generating information such as financials is a complex task unless each partner is prepared to provide the other with budget information when it is needed and in a format that the partner can recognize. There are numerous examples of information flow conflicts that must be resolved. The Decision-Making Analysis tool identifies these conflicts and allows managers to adapt.

Tool 6: Expectation Mapping

Expectation Mapping is the final tool that should be used during the Implementation Plan workshops. This tool is designed to help counterparts on each side identify their expectations and accurately communicate them on a one-to-one level. As pointed out in Chapter 6, an alliance is often compared to a marriage. As well as being relationships between institutions, alliances, like marriages, are relationships between individuals. Therefore, the forces that build strong relationships between individuals have a powerful effect on alliances. Marriage counselors understand these forces and how to use them. Before applying any such advice, it is important to understand the anatomy of an alliance.

The Anatomy of an Alliance. During the early days of an alliance, the primary communication channel between firms is typically from Implementation Team to Implementation Team, as shown in Figure 9-4. The Implementation Team in each firm is composed of members from the stakeholder organizations that will contribute resources to the relationship. Each team is led by an alliance Operating Manager who in turn reports to an Alliance Executive. The Implementation Teams have the dual responsibility of ensuring that internal groups provide their resources to the alliance, as well as coordinating the two firms' efforts internally and externally.

Figure 9-4. Anatomy of an alliance: the early days.

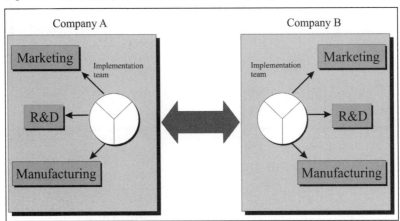

As the alliance matures, a second communication channel emerges and overlays itself upon the first. The first channel does not go away. Rather, the two coexist and form the complete mature communication structure of the alliance. The second channel develops as key members of each functional group identify their counterparts in the partner company and build a working relationship (see Figure 9-5). For example, a marketing group leader in Company A identifies her counterpart in Company B.

They form a functional pair. A research scientist in Company A and her counterpart in Company B identify each other and form a functional pair. There may be ten to fifteen such pairs in an alliance. Getting these functional pairs to work together effectively is critical to implementation success.

Figure 9-5. Anatomy of an alliance: the mature alliance.

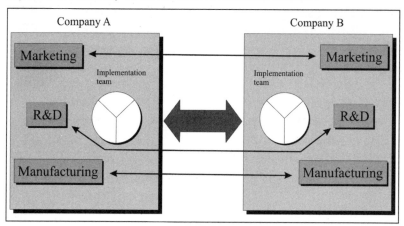

The vitality of an alliance resides in the health of ten to fifteen key functional pairs.

Alliance Operating Managers can significantly improve the probability of success by maintaining the health of these key functional pairs. The challenge is to identify the pairs early, clearly outline the roles and responsibilities of each person, and help them build the interpersonal relationships that allow them to function smoothly and effectively. The Expectation Mapping tool is designed to do that.

Expectation Mapping: Defining Roles and Responsibilities at the Individual Contributor Level

Marriage counselors know that when two individuals agree on key expectations of a relationship, they focus their energy on achieving mutual goals. The same is true for functional pairs. Expectation Mapping ensures that people begin a working relationship with a clear understanding of their respective roles, responsibilities, and accountability.

Without the Expectation Mapping process, newly formed pairs spend the early days of the alliance stumbling through a clumsy process of figuring out who will do what, who will bring what resources, and when specific deliverables are expected. These trial-and-error interactions are frustrating when people know their roles exactly and think they know their counterpart's roles exactly. Problems arise because they don't agree on those roles, and they are unaware that they don't agree. The larger the unknown disagreement, the larger the conflict. When one functional pair suffers a disconnect, the alliance suffers. When multiple pairs suffer misunderstandings, the alliance is at risk.

Expectation Mapping at the Operating Manager Level

Expectation Mapping is particularly important at the Operating Manager level. When these men and women mentally stake out their areas of responsibility, they become protective of their turf. Problems arise when two managers stake out the same turf but don't know it. Figure 9-6 illustrates the situation in which the managers from companies A and B each identify their area of responsibility and mentally draw a boundary around it. Both managers have unique areas of responsibility, but they have unknowingly carved out the same space in the shaded area (R). Confusion results when these managers send conflicting messages to their subordinates. Frustration emerges when Implementation Team members find others "doing my job." Since the root of the problem is not understood, the solution cannot be identified.

Figure 9-6. Expectation Mapping.

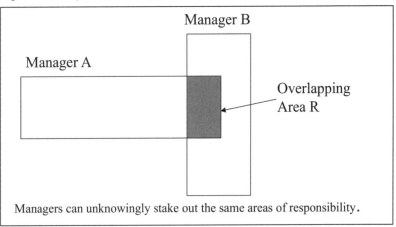

Managers can unknowingly stake out the same areas of responsibility.

Expectation Mapping as a New Member Socialization Tool

Expectation Mapping has advantages that go far beyond allowing counterparts to gain consensus. It is a powerful tool for socializing new members into the alliance. When a new person replaces a functional pair member, a warning flag goes up. Sometimes the new person reestablishes the prior relationship quickly and efficiently. Sometimes they do not. Expectation Mapping is an excellent tool to socialize new members quickly.

Smart Operating Managers use Expectation Mapping on a regular basis. Some ask key functional pairs to map their expectations every six months or once a year. Whatever the appropriate time frame, it becomes a method for ensuring openness, honesty, and constructive feedback into the alliance.

FILLING OUT THE EXPECTATION MAPPING TOOL

Both members of a functional pair fill out the Expectation Mapping tool, shown in Figure 9-7, twice. First, each person describes the tasks he or she will perform, when the task will be performed, and the required deliverables. They give a clear and accurate description of their roles, responsibilities, accountabilities, and authority. Then each person fills out the same form describing his or her counterpart. The members of each functional pair share the forms and discuss areas of agreement and disagreement. If the pair cannot agree on particular issues, they bring their questions to management for resolution. The final result of Expectation Mapping is a clearly defined working relationship between functional pair members.

Figure 9-7. Expectation Mapping worksheet.

What tasks must be performed?
If a task requires the partner's cooperation, list each person's key responsibilities.

Task 1: _____ Date needed: _____

Deliverable:_____

Key responsibilities:
Company A team member   Company B team member

_____   _____

_____   _____

_____   _____

Task 2: _____ Date needed: _____

Deliverable:_____

Key responsibilities:
Company A team member   Company B team member

_____   _____

_____   _____

_____   _____

Level of organizational responsibility:

• Roles _____

• Responsibility _____

• Accountability _____

• Authority _____

Each functional pair member fills out the form twice—once for himself/herself and once for the counterpart.

Tips for Implementing the Alliance

To improve your chances of success, follow these tips:

- Introduce the alliance Operating Manager in your partner firm to the tools in this chapter.
- Jointly decide which tools make sense for your alliance.
- Integrate the selected tools into the normal workflow of the alliance.
- Discuss the members of your Implementation Team with your partner firm, with special emphasis on identifying functional pairs.
- Minimize rotating employees through the positions held by key functional pair members. When a change of personnel must be made, use Expectation Mapping to help reform the functional pair.
- Use the characteristics of the alliance Operating Manager, described in this chapter, as a guideline for filling this key position.
- Use the following six tools, which are intended to help you cross organizational boundaries:

  1. Joint Negotiator Presentation
  2. Intellectual Property Disclosure Rules
  3. Implementation Plan Workshops
  4. Stakeholder Mapping
  5. Decision-Making Analysis
  6. Expectation Mapping

While these first six AIP tools help Operating Managers coordinate and integrate the skills and resources across organizational boundaries, they are not perfect. Conflict often results as a normal and natural part of every collaborative relationship. The next chapter explores the nature of conflict and provides managers with six additional tools to deal with this complex aspect of alliance management.

Notes

1. Nelson Sims, Roger Harrison, and Anton Gueth, "Managing Alliances at Lilly," *In Vivo* (June 2001), pp. 71–77.
2. M. D. Cohen, J. G. March, and J. P. Olsen, "A Garbage Can Model of Organizational Choice," *Administrative Sciences Quarterly* 17 (1972), pp. 1–25.

MANAGING CONFLICT

Alliance Operating Managers need to be a little neurotic. The fact that over half of all alliances fail is not all bad. Some failure is normal, even valuable as firms undertake projects with risk profiles outside their normal comfort range. When "intelligent risk" results in "intelligent failure," the firm can move ahead a little smarter for having gone through the experience. "Dumb failure" is another story. When a strategic opportunity is squandered because the partners cannot coordinate and integrate their resources, value is frittered away. There can be a fine line between "intelligent" and "dumb" failure. Operating Managers cross the line when they take a reactive stance to dealing with conflict.

Implementation Team members become emotionally invested in an alliance. Conflict is an expression of that investment. Experienced firms prepare their alliance participants to deal with conflict, minimize its impact, and extract the organizational learning that every conflict offers. Properly managed, issues that lead to friction are identified early and resolved. Alliance Operating Managers harvest the positive outcomes of constructive conflict and turn a negative into a positive.

The Alliance Implementation Program (AIP) highlights the importance of conflict resolution and provides managers with six tools specifically designed to manage conflict. The purpose of this chapter is to outline those tools.

What Is Conflict?

Conflict is defined as the existence of competing or incompatible options to reach a single goal or objective.[1] Conflict does not imply hostility, although hostility is often a part of the process. Rather, conflict propels a group toward the goal when it enhances creativity, builds interteam cohesion, and leads to problem identification and solution generation.

Alliances require change. Change means movement. Movement means friction. A common misconception about conflict is that if left alone, it will resolve itself. Wrong! Conflict loves to be ignored. While managers stand by and hope the problem will go away, conflict festers, gains momentum, impacts unrelated issues, and leads to all sorts of unhealthy behaviors. Left unmanaged, conflict strains relationships, decreases productivity, erodes trust, and leads to an "us vs. them" mind-set characterized by decision-making paralysis.

Lack of attention to this issue will bring an alliance

to its knees. Conflict remains unmanaged because people on both sides believe that confronting issues is unpleasant. Behavior not confronted will not change. Talk to the marriage counselors. Talk to the psychologists. Many people who are behaving badly do not know they are doing anything disturbing, and they have no idea that their behavior is damaging the alliance.

The only thing worse than confronting conflict is not confronting it.

Why Conflict Quietly Gets Worse

While Operating Managers patiently wait for conflict to go away, it quietly transforms itself from an accumulation of half-remembered and relatively minor truths to a major conspiracy compounded by each person's perception of who did what to whom and when. It's not long before the people involved are not even sure what the conflict is really about.

Once people dig in their heels on an issue they are trapped. It is difficult for people to reverse their position and admit they are wrong. The need to be consistent, coupled with the need to be right, makes saving face an important factor. Many long-standing conflicts have nothing to do with the original issues. The real conflict is a complicated chess game where the goal is to withdraw with honor.

Personality characteristics complicate the picture. Some people avoid conflict at all costs. Others will argue over anything. The art of "picking your battles" combined with the ability to compromise are important coping skills in alliances. They focus attention on conflicts worth pursuing, rather than on endless unproductive discussions. Experienced managers know that once a problem is identified, well defined, and acknowledged, it is half solved. The art of conflict management is helping people decouple their egos from the challenges they face.

The Three Stages of Conflict

When managers demystify the concept of conflict and lay it on the table for Implementation Team members to examine, good things happen. People are able to recognize when they are entering into a conflict scenario and take action. By applying the tools in this chapter, positive outcomes emerge from negative situations and losers become winners. It all starts with an understanding of the "three stages of conflict."

- *Stage 1 conflict* is characterized by low-intensity, day-to-day irritations. These events are no big deal. They are coped with easily, simply ignored, or sloughed off as unimportant. Facts and opinions are shared openly among people with a disagreement. Participants seek solutions to problems. Most conflict never gets past this stage.

- *Stage 2 conflict* takes on an aura of competition and is characterized by a growing win-lose attitude. Self-interest and saving face take on new importance as people become the problem. Witnesses take sides. The participants keep track of victories and record mistakes. A sober discussion of the issues is difficult because people are as concerned with personality issues as they are with facts. Complexity increases quickly as people withhold information from each other.

Stage 2 conflict left unaddressed will magnify any problem. Yet it is difficult to deal with conflict at this stage because issues and individuals' emotions have become intertwined. The level of effort required to work through stage 2 conflict is significantly higher than in stage 1. One technique that helps is to have each side describe the worst-case scenario from both an organizational and individual career perspective. People are shocked by the effect of the worst-case scenario on the organization and their personal goals. That shock can drive the conflict back to stage 1, where a calmer atmosphere facilitates solution.

● *Stage 3 conflict* is all-out war. It is almost impossible for people to refocus their energies on the goals of the alliance. The objective is not to solve the problem but to hurt the other side. Every conflict has a history and people immerse themselves in emotional discussions of who did what to whom. No one talks about the solution. Threats and counterthreats are common. Logic and reason are not effective at dissuading others. If the conflict reaches this stage, the alliance is probably over. Without serious third-party intervention, the best each side can hope for is the efficient breakup of the relationship. Arbitration, mediation, and litigation are common methods to deal with stage 3 conflict. The lawyers get rich and competitors take advantage of the chaos.

The Six Tools to Overcome Conflict

Tool 7: The Conflict Prediction Tool

The value of resolving conflict in stage 1 is clear. The Conflict Prediction Tool (CPT) helps alliance Operating Managers to predict where and how partner firms will have trouble integrating resources. It also suggests pre-emptive actions to avoid alliance damage. Like the other tools in the Alliance Implementation Program, the CPT should be used at the appropriate organizational level. For the CPT, that is the level where resource integration must happen. For example, in a multinational pharmaceutical alliance involving the co-promotion of a drug in multiple countries, the CPT might be applied to marketing departments in each firm on a country-by-country basis. In a collaborative R&D relationship between a large and small firm, the CPT could be used between the relevant R&D department of the large firm and the entire R&D organization of the small firm.

There is no coming back from stage 3 conflict. Once a cucumber becomes a pickle, it can never be a cucumber again.

The Conflict Prediction Tool requires Implementation Team stakeholder representatives to predict where resource integration difficulties are likely to occur, based on the past performance of the groups inside each stakeholder organization. The Conflict Prediction Tool (see Figure 10-1) captures the views of the stakeholder representatives and presents them to the alliance Operating Managers for action. The simplest way to use the tool is to ask stakeholder representatives to predict where resource integration will go well and where it will falter. By combining the predictions of Implementation Team members from corresponding stakeholder groups of each partner, a pattern emerges that suggests areas for the Operating Managers' attention. Once potential resource integration issues are identified, the Operating Managers work with the stakeholder representatives and other line managers from both partners to head off problems before they begin to cause damage. For example, a predicted R&D integration issue might be addressed by facilitated discussions among first-level managers and leading scientists from both partners who are focused on how they will work together and share information and ideas.

The downside of being a great alliance manager is that you start sounding like your mother—play nice, share your toys, listen to your neighbor, don't bite.

The Conflict Prediction Tool must be used with care and awareness of people's personal and cultural sensitivities, since it predicts and deals with problems that are yet to arise in the alliance. Its use is a perfect example of the talents required of alliance Operating Managers (described in Chapter 9). The downside of the CPT is that it works too well. By predicting problems and solving them early, resource integration issues never arise and the damage never happens. To someone not close to the situ-

Figure 10-1. Conflict Prediction Tool.

(To be filled out by stakeholders in both firms)

- Please predict the four areas of resource integration that will *not* go smoothly during the alliance.

    1. _____

    2. _____

    3. _____

    4. _____

- What recomendations can you make to resolve these difficulties?

    _____

    _____

ation, it looks like the Implementation Team wasted time solving a nonissue. Don't be deterred. This is a very effective tool that can help prevent derailment.

Great alliance Operating Managers make it look easy because they solve problems before they occur.

Tool 8: Breakdown Sessions

Breakdown sessions are the eighth tool of the Alliance Implementation Program. These sessions are also designed to prevent problems before they occur. Most conflicts in organizations fester for months before they surface to do their damage. Part of the delay is caused by the difficulty of identifying potential conflicts early. Part of the delay stems from people's reluctance to raise unpleasant issues with counterparts. Human nature makes it difficult to bring up sensitive subjects or hurt another's feelings. Mature adults have been socialized to smile at others, respect their opinions, and be polite. Dwelling on problems, pointing out mistakes, and complaining about poor performance flies in the face of everything we were taught as children. Yet that level of open and honest discussion is exactly what is needed for the smooth functioning of the alliance.

Marriage counselors are black belts in preventing conflict. They start with a philosophy that sunlight is the best disinfectant, and they work hard to help the parties identify issues and seek multiple solutions. Breakdown sessions serve this function in alliances. Their purpose is to surface issues that may cause friction between the parties in a nonthreatening way and to do it early, in stage 1 of the conflict process. Here's how the process works.

- *Use quarterly meetings to identify future conflicts.* Most alliances use quarterly meetings to bring the Implementation Teams together and gauge progress. Breakdown sessions should be held at each quarterly meeting. Ask Implementation Team members from both firms to devote thirty minutes to a discussion of the issues that may cause friction between the partners during the next three months. This meeting is not the time to rehash old problems or discuss current issues. The breakdown session is reserved for looking into the future and identifying likely friction points. For example, discuss the deliverables for the next quarter. What barriers stand in the way? Which organizations in each partner firm must provide resources, and what resource limitations are suspected to exist? What decisions must be made, and is there a potential for delay in that decision-making process? By exploring the alliance agenda over the next three months with an eye toward identifying friction points, the Implementation Team quickly identifies stage 1 issues. The value of the breakdown session is that it provides a regular, ongoing opportunity for Implementation Team members to raise issues of concern before damage is done. It allows everyone to calmly discuss future problems that are awkward to raise in other venues.

● *Set the ground rules.* It is best to conduct the breakdown session under a set of simple ground rules. Remind members of the Implementation Team that the purpose of the session is to identify future areas of potential friction. Encourage them to speak in personal terms using "I" statements rather than attacking others. Reinforce the notion that the goal of the session is to have a rational discussion of possible friction points. View assumptions skeptically. Too often, people adopt their view of the partner's organization as fact. Closer examination shows that a limited understanding of the partner's organizational structure and political network leads to fundamentally flawed views of the partner's intent. Finally, deal with rumors or accusations directly. Rumors abound in alliances, and accusations usually follow. The most effective way to deal with these alliance killers is face-to-face interaction focused on specific issues.

● *Encourage participation.* The most difficult part of the process is encouraging people to participate the first time. Team members do not want to be seen as complainers or predictors of trouble not yet proven to exist. The alliance Operating Managers from both companies should encourage participation by actively participating in the process themselves and by expressing their support for constructive criticism, which has value in defusing conflict in stage 1.

● *Use a third-party facilitator.* Using a third-party facilitator to lead the breakdown session is helpful during the first few quarterly meetings. Some firms use members of their human resources (HR) staff to facilitate breakdown sessions. That works best when HR people from both firms participate, because neither firm is seen as biasing the process. The Implementation Team may benefit from having a third-party facilitator who is experienced in alliances. It is a rare event that alliances develop problems that have never been seen before. Most conflicts are identifiable, predictable, and have been repeated in thousands of relationships. If the facilitator is an experienced alliance professional, he or she can provide value beyond the simple facilitation process. The facilitator may even be able to help build trust.

Tool 9: The Trust Self-Assessment Tool

Trust is a fundamental human value that shapes our behavior, guides our decision making, and lowers our defenses. Every manager knows it is important to build trust into an alliance, but few know how to do it. Managers believe that the bonds of trust emerge from meeting obligations and being open with the partner. That's part of it. However, managing toward these simple concepts will not build trust into an alliance. To leverage the power of trust in interpersonal relationships, trust must be built into the fabric of the relationship through continual reinforcement. It must be focused, managed, nurtured, and rewarded.

Psychologists spent years understanding the concept of trust. The best psychologists thought past the basic concept and spent quality time exploring its roots. By answering questions such as "What are the antecedents of trust?" and "What psychological mechanisms lead to the granting or withdrawal of trust?" they developed insights that managers can use to proactively institutionalize trust into the alliance.

Their conclusions can be briefly summarized. When one person decides to grant another the gift of trust in a working relationship, a calculation goes on in the mind. The person granting the honor of trust evaluates the other person along four dimensions:

1. *Competence.* Does the person have the skills necessary to accomplish the task?
2. *Reliability.* Does the person deliver what is expected, when it is expected, and in the form it is expected?
3. *Open/Honest Communications.* Is the person forthright in his or her dealings?
4. *Caring.* Is this person willing to defend the interests of the other, even when that defense negatively affects his or her own interests?

If the person scores very low on any one dimension, trust is withheld. The higher the person scores on each dimension, the stronger the bond. Think about it. If

someone is competent, reliable, honest, and willing to
risk their career for you, what's not to like about them?
Take a moment to review the Trust Self-Assessment Tool
in Figure 10-2. It transforms these fundamental insights
into a tool for alliance management.

Figure 10-2. Trust Self-Assessment Tool.

● How would my counterpart in the partner firm rate me on the four characteristics of trust?						
— Competence						
1	2	3	4	5	6	7
— Reliability						
1	2	3	4	5	6	7
— Honesty						
1	2	3	4	5	6	7
— Caring						
1	2	3	4	5	6	7
NOTE: 1=High 4=Average 7=Needs Improvement						

As the name suggests, the Trust Self-Assessment is
intended for use only by an individual for assessing him-
self or herself. This minimizes personal anxiety. Here's
how it works: Each alliance Operating Manager provides
the tool to members of the team or other alliance participants twice a year. The Operating Manager should
encourage people to review their behavior from the partner's perspective, asking questions such as: Have I been

open and honest in my dealings with the partner? Have I reliably delivered the work products expected of me in a quality manner? Do I have the competencies needed to perform my role? Have I taken the time to care for my counterpart in the partner firm?

The results are the property of the person doing the self-assessment. The individual must then decide whether to share the results with other Implementation Team members or the person's counterpart in the partner firm. The power of the tool comes from its use by individuals, not through sharing the results. Operating Managers should use the Trust Self-Assessment Tool with sensitivity. Overuse can lead to staleness and a "going through the motions" process.

Further Thoughts on the Caring Dimension of Trust. Ask any manager about the four dimensions of trust, and they usually place competence, reliability, and honesty on the list. However, caring is a different issue. When you ask people in an alliance how they show caring for their counterparts in the partner firm, you get some interesting answers. A typical response is: "Implementation Team members should listen to the partner's views, think about issues from their perspective, and include the partner in all decision making." But that answer does not go deep enough. Caring in alliances means taking risks—even risks that threaten one's own standing in the firm. If members of the Implementation Team are not protecting the partner's interests within the firm, who is? We have a metric for determining how well someone is caring for the partner. It is called the "great Implementation Team member test." If someone's boss yells, "Who do you work for, us or them?" that person is a great Implementation Team member. Chances are that person is working to protect the partner and arguing for the best outcome for the alliance, not necessarily for her firm.

That's quite a risk. And it leads to the next question: What is the career path of a great Implementation Team member, or a great alliance Operating Manager? Take another look at Figure 10-2. While this individual is building trust inside the partner's firm, she may be eroding it in her own company. Senior executives may question the reliability of her decisions. Counterparts may question her commitment to the firm and wonder if she has "gone native" because she sides with the partner on key issues. Her openness and honesty may become a question mark if she's perceived as placing the best interests of the partner firm ahead of her own firm.

What is the actual effect of caring on the careers of Implementation Team members and Operating Managers? Where do these people go? No one knows the answer. Some believe the path is up through management to greater levels of responsibility. Others believe the path is out the door to work for the partner or another firm. Whatever the answer, it is important for every person working in the alliance to make a sober assessment of the role the alliance will play in his or her career. Alliances and careers are tightly linked. A person's performance on any unusual project receives extra visibility. Behaviors that disappear into the background on in-house projects are highlighted in alliances. Views on a person's performance come from a new angle as the partner shares perceptions with in-house management.

Tool 10: Technology Transfer Questions

In their simplest form, alliances are mechanisms for transferring technology across organizational boundaries.

For the purposes of this discussion, we will define "technology" broadly to include information of all types, including specialized skill sets, technical know-how, marketing know-how, physical assets, and business practices. Whatever the technology being transferred, the physical act of transfer is a subject that encourages lively debate. Dozens of books and more than one journal on the topic signal the level of complexity and its importance. Central to the debate is what practices work best when one firm sends technology to another, and what steps managers must take to prepare themselves to accept the technology of another. An example will help frame the question.

Think about purchasing two high-tech products: a halogen lightbulb and a computer database program. What are the issues that allow the manufacturer to successfully transfer that technology to you? The easiest transfer is the lightbulb. Simply unscrew the old bulb, screw in the new one, and turn on the switch. That flawless transfer of high technology is possible because you did not have to learn anything. You already knew how to change a lightbulb.

Contrast that with using a database program. Install it on your computer. Boot it up. Try to create a database, build a data file, and use the search function. The process is daunting because new knowledge must be acquired at every step. Does it have to be that way? Some extent of learning will always be required, but sophisticated manufacturers understand the value of creating user-friendly products; products whose functions are intuitively easy to use and mimic well-known routines.

What does this have to do with alliances? Everything. Successful alliance partners develop "user-friendly" transfer processes. They transfer halogen lightbulbs, not database programs. When the firm sending the technology knows how the partner will receive it and how it will be used, the sending firm can tailor its transfer process to maximize ease of use. Similarly, the receiving firm maximizes its ability to receive by understanding the processes of the sending firm.

Sending the equivalent of halogen lightbulbs reduces frustration and decreases cycle time. In one biotechnology alliance between a large and small firm, the small firm sent samples of molecules to the large firm for testing. The scientists from the small firm had developed a shorthand notation for describing what was in the sample container and who had prepared the sample. They labeled each container using their proprietary notation.

The scientists at the large firm did not recognize the hieroglyphics, but did not ask for clarification because they did not want to seem ignorant. The small firm's technology was part of the latest trend in molecular biology, and the large firm's scientists wanted their small firm counterparts to believe that the large firm was on the cutting edge. To figure out the meanings of the container notations, the large firm's scientists searched the scientific literature. Nothing. Next they called leading academic researchers. Still no clue. Finally, they ran a series of laboratory tests to determine the contents, with only partial success. Weeks later an informal phone call revealed that the small firm was using a proprietary notation, and the issue was resolved. The moral of this story? Use the Technology Transfer Questions listed in Figure 10-3 to understand the related issues most likely to affect the alliance. Spend time understanding how each firm sends and receives information relevant to the alliance. The two Implementation Teams must jointly develop user-friendly methods of technology transfer.

Figure 10-3. Technology Transfer Questions.

- What technology must we transfer to the partner over the next 3, 6, and 12 months?
- How will they use that technology?
- What do we need to learn about the partner's operation to more effectively transfer this technology to them?
- What must they learn about our operations to more effectively receive the technology from us?
- What organizational barriers stand in our/their way?
- Whose help must we enlist in our/their firm to overcome these organizational barriers?

Tool 11: Arguing the Partner's Position

Crossing the no-man's-land of conflict is an art, not a science. Masters of this art form understand that conflict results when two well-meaning people develop rational but mutually exclusive solutions to the same problem. Sometimes compromise or capitulation will resolve alliance conflicts and the partners move on. However, when each person strongly believes that his position is the best solution for solving a problem, conflict results. Resolution becomes increasingly difficult if the conflict moves beyond stage 1.

The governance structure of the alliance is the final arbitrator of ongoing disputes. As discussed in Chapter 8, the governance structure usually includes an interpartner steering committee made up of top executives that deals with especially contentious issues. However, a steering committee can only deal with a dispute it fully understands. Fragmented fact patterns, biased information sources, and an incomplete understanding of the organizational context that surrounds the dispute all conspire to mislead even the most objective top executives. One solution is to ask the alliance Operating Manager from each firm to write two one-page descriptions of the dispute, one from her own persepctive and one based on her view of the partner's perspective. The two Operating Managers then exchange both one-page descriptions and discuss the differences. The first benefit of this technique is that it enables the two Operating Managers to get a better understanding of the dispute, which may lead to a mutually acceptable solution. Another advantage is that the steering committee can assess how far apart the parties are on key aspects of the dispute, and how various options for resolution will affect the alliance and each partner firm.

The simple act of writing down each firm's position often suggests possibilities for resolution that neither Operating Manager thought of when viewing the dispute from his own position. It also acts as the final opportunity for resolution at the operating level. When successive large disputes or too many small disputes need arbitration at the steering committee level, a review of the operating policies of the alliance is in order. The question is, "What is preventing managers at the operating level from resolving alliance issues?" As experienced Operating Managers will tell you, "When problems start going to the steering committee, the alliance was over long ago."

Tool 12: Valuing the Partner's Contribution

Looking past the obvious sources of conflict and identifying its underlying cause is the realm of the psychologist.

Family therapists and marriage counselors have long understood that couples argue about trivial matters as a surrogate for the deeper issues that separate them. Take the common marital dispute of "who does what" around the house. Hardworking couples come home to a sink full of dishes, babies that need changing, and piles of laundry. The chores seem thankless—and endless. Arguments start out with statements such as "I always" and "You never." Each side develops long lists of accomplishments as proof of how much they contribute. Neither hears the other as frustrations deepen.

What the arguing spouses do not understand is that their dispute has nothing to do with work, or family, or effort. It has to do with the need to feel cherished. People don't ask for much in this life. A universal desire is to have one's efforts appreciated by another. Husbands and wives joyfully go about mundane tasks if they know that the other understands, appreciates, and cherishes the effort.

Take a moment to cherish the efforts of the alliance partner. Send them a card for a job well done. Create a "Non-Employee of the Month" award and give it to a top performer in the partner firm. Have the local pizzeria deliver a double cheese and pepperoni deluxe to the partner's door. No reason, just send the pizza. These small acts are the "sticky stuff" that glues partners together.

Using the AIP Tools in a Supportive Organization

Team members carry out their work within the larger context of the firm. Some firms have institutionalized formal alliance processes. Most have not. In either case, the tools of the Alliance Implementation Program must be viewed in the context of the larger organization. How do they integrate with other established tools, policies, and procedures? What can managers do to share information learned across alliances? What metrics are important and when should they be used? The purpose of the next chapter is to follow three companies as they attempt to answer these questions. As you will see, each firm approached the problem from its unique perspective, and each developed a different solution. But each solution was right for the company involved. In Chapter 11 we follow these three companies—Eli Lilly and Company, Procter & Gamble Pharmaceuticals, and Air Products and Chemicals, Inc.— as they institutionalize alliance management into their firm.

Tips on Managing Conflict

Conflict is inevitable when implementing an alliance. Here are a few things to remember:

- Add information about the three stages of conflict to your alliance training program.
- Use the Conflict Prediction Tool to identify potential areas of conflict before the alliance begins.
- Confront unpleasant issues, however difficult. Management can use breakdown sessions to identify potential conflicts before they arise. Managers who ignore conflict and hope it will go away miss the opportunity to resolve conflict during stage 1.
- Apply the six conflict resolution tools during quarterly meetings as a way to minimize conflict in the alliance.

- Have alliance Operating Managers set an example for other Implementation Team members by actively applying these tools to the relationship.
- Make it easier to transfer technology between partners by fostering a clear understanding of how the technology is used by the sender and how it will be used by the receiver.
- Use the following Alliance Implementation Program tools to help deal with conflict:

Conflict Prediction Tool

Breakdown Sessions

Trust Self-Assessment Tool

Technology Transfer Questions

Arguing the Partner's Position

Valuing the Partner's Contribution

Notes

1. We are indebted to Peg Pickering's *How to Manage Conflict* (Franklin Lakes, NJ: Career Press, 2000) for this definition and her lucid description of conflict that forms the basis of this section.

C H A P T E R   1 1

ALLIANCE
MANAGEMENT SYSTEMS
AND ALLIANCE
METRICS

How do you measure alliance success? What are leading firms doing to institutionalize alliance management into the firm? What are the key elements to measure? Leading alliance companies have developed answers to these complex questions. In this chapter, we will follow managers in Eli Lilly and Company, Air Products and Chemicals, Inc., and Procter & Gamble Pharmaceuticals as they address these issues. But first, it is instructive to look at the fundamental requirements that should guide the architects of any alliance management system.

The Requirements of an Alliance Management System

People who study the history of organizations gain insights on emerging patterns in effective management. One pattern is the powerful effect of institutionalizing processes that were developed as a result of important corporate initiatives. In this context, "institutionalizing" does not mean casting policies or procedures in bureaucratic stone. Rather, it means unlocking hard-won knowledge that resides in the minds of a few, and making that knowledge available to many.

That pattern is emerging in alliances. Historically, individuals in companies gain expertise in alliance management the hard way, by making mistakes and learning from them. When those individuals leave or move on to other jobs, the knowledge is lost. Their successors, or people with alliance responsibilities elsewhere in the firm, make the same mistakes over and over again. Aware of that history, some firms are creating alliance management systems that deliver skills and knowledge to each alliance. These systems are evolving as firms find the optimum balance between system costs and benefits.

While the Alliance Framework and the Alliance Implementation Program are useful components of a complete alliance management system, there is no one best system that will work in every company. However, an effective alliance management system should have the following eight characteristics. It must be:

1. Complete
2. Widely applicable
3. Flexible

4. Stakeholder created
5. Learnable
6. Improvable
7. Top-management supported
8. Connected

Let's look at each characteristic more carefully:

● *A Complete System.* The system must include components that cover the entire alliance formation and implementation life cycle, including: the preparation of a short list of potential partners; partner evaluation and selection; preparation for and conduct of negotiations; the actual process of negotiating the deal; start-up issues; conflict resolution; continuous improvement; and transfer of learnings to other alliances.

Measurement systems are essential and must provide alliance Operating Managers with the tools they need to diagnose and improve the performance of their alliance. The measurement systems may also provide top management with a clear understanding of the costs and benefits of each individual alliance as well as the value of the entire alliance portfolio.

● *A Widely Applicable System.* The system must be applicable to any alliance situation. Alliances may range from small relationships, such as limited geography distribution agreements or in-licensing of single patents, to large multiparty global technology development, manufacturing, and marketing alliances. The system must be applicable to the entire portfolio of relationships, not simply a subset. However, the system must balance this breadth with scalability. Certain system tools will be applicable to every alliance while others may meet the complex needs of only a few.

● *A Flexible System.* The system must be applicable at any step of the alliance life cycle. The system must be adaptable to variations in management style and organizational structure. It must also be adaptable to the styles of many different potential partners. The optimum system will incorporate feedback loops to allow for changing circumstances within either firm or in the external business environment. These loops not only identify areas that need attention, but also suggest action items for management follow-up.

● *A Stakeholder-Created System.* The stakeholders who will use the system should create the system. While the starting point must include components of demonstrated value, the detailed configuration of components and the overall system should reflect the creative inputs of stakeholders. Systems that are mandated by top management, and often developed by external consultants, have a history of failure. It is better to have the people who face the problems develop the solutions. Given proper external support, stakeholders are likely to develop a user-friendly system that meets their needs.

● *A Learnable System.* The system must be understood and used by people of varied backgrounds and levels of alliance experience. This requirement acknowledges the need for guidance by experts in alliances, but emphasizes the need for just-in-time (JIT) learning. JIT systems provide people with needed information when they need it, in an easy-to-use format. Chapter 9 identified a goal of using less than 3 percent of a person's time to deliver greater than 50 percent improvement in the performance of the relationship. Using this metric as a guideline, the system must be intuitive, provide immediate value, and be very easy to use. Anything less will be ignored by managers who must spend their scarce resources achieving alliance objectives. The system should include training and support to enable people to use system components effectively.

- *An Improvable System.* Each component and the overall system must be improvable based on the experience of the organization. A designated group within the firm, usually including the business development and legal departments, working with stakeholder organizations, should drive improvements.

- *A Top Management–Supported System.* The system must receive top management support for its development and implementation, with adequate resource commitments and alliance decision-making processes tied to the system.

- *A Connected System.* Components of the system that generate data and information should be electronically integrated into the firm's overall information architecture.

Air Products and Chemicals' Alliance Portfolio Measurement System

How can a firm with dozens of alliances estimate the value of the portfolio? How can that information help management allocate resources between internal projects and external alliances? Can a measurement system be created that is easy to use and flexible? Dr. John Tao and Merrill Brenner developed a tool (see Figure 11-1) to answer these questions and measure the potential impact of external research projects. When the tool is used in conjunction with five- to ten-minute interviews with the technical project champion, it becomes a powerful method to measure the impact of a top-rated project on the bottom line. Executives at Air Products and Chemicals use this tool to help them allocate resources to projects.

Air Products and Chemicals is a $5.5 billion global company producing industrial and specialty gases and chemicals. Roughly 6 percent of its $130 million R&D budget is spent in collaboration with external partners. Those external research projects are saving an average of two years of internal effort for each external project undertaken, plus hundreds of thousands of dollars of net research expenditures. External research projects also offer a potential revenue increase of tens of millions of dollars per year, or a profit increase of millions of dollars per year. How do they know all this? They measure it using a rating tool for evaluating alliances.

Through 2001, John Tao and Merrill Brenner evaluated forty-two external projects using this rating tool. In the following sections, each component of their evaluation process and scoring system is explained.[1]

Three Project Phases

The first question in the evaluation is: How does each alliance executive categorize the phase of the external technology development project? A project is categorized as phase 1 when the external partner makes the major

Figure 11-1. Rating tool for projecting the impact of external research projects.

Stage	New Idea	New Expertise, Skills, Capabilities	Time Saved	Net R&D $ Saved	Background IP Access	IP Generation	Long-Term Access to Capabilities	Program Emphasis	Rating (4)	Commercial Impact	Technical Leverage
External Technology Research (1)											
Internal Technology Research (2)											
Application/ Process Development/ Commercialization Rating (3)											
3	Scientific advance	World-class fundamental understanding	>Two years	>= $1 MM	Lot or exclusive & royalty-free	Dominating	>$200 MM or high breadth & depth	Offensive/ critical	5	>$50 MM sales or $7 MM savings; e.g., new business or new process	Blockbuster
2	Novel technology	Unique skill or know-how	1–2 years	$100 Ks	Exclusive/ low royalty or nonexclusive/ free	Extension	$20–$200 MM or high breadth or depth	Defensive/ critical	3	$10–$50 MM sales or $1–$7 MM savings; e.g., new product line or major process change	Major advance
1	New wrinkle	Unique capability	Months	$10 Ks	Little or nonexclusive & royalty	Incremental	<$20 MM or moderate depth &/or breadth	Offensive or defensive and not critical	2	$1–$10 MM sales or $0.1–$1 MM savings; e.g., new product or incremental process improvement	Incremental
0	Idea undefined	Outsourced labor	<One month	<= 0	None	None	Small or specific capabilities	Maintenance	1	<$1 MM sales or $0.1 MM savings	Straight-forward

NOTES:
(1) Evaluation of external development   (3) Scale for first eight characteristics across top
(2) Use of external development   (4) Scale for Commercial Impact and Technical Leverage

SOURCE: Merrill S. Brenner and John C. Tao, "You Can Measure External Research Programs," in *Research★Technology Management* (May–June 2001), pp. 14–17. Reprinted with permission.

effort; phase 2 when it is a joint program; and phase 3 when Air Products and Chemicals, Inc. performs the bulk of the work. This helps clarify the extent to which the external research project is actually external.

Project Characterization

The next step is to assess the project according to a list of characteristics (see Figure 11-1). The project is assigned a score ranging from zero to three for each characteristic.

The first characteristic categorizes the project using a "novelty" criterion. A project based on a new scientific advance is scored as a three. A lower score is assigned to new technology based on a well-understood science, and a still lower score for a new wrinkle on existing technology. A zero score is assigned to a project that does not depend on new science or technology. The novelty criterion is both a rough measure of the possible impact of the project and the risk associated with it.

The next two characteristics, which describe the strategic value of the project to the company, are in the Program Emphasis column. Air Products uses terms such as "offensive," which is applied to a project that establishes a new product opportunity, or "defensive," which is aimed at protecting the market position of an existing product. The project is also characterized as "critical" or "not critical" based on the degree to which a product depends on project success.

Each project is also assessed on the following characteristics, again using the zero to three scale (zero meaning minimal impact, three meaning significant impact):

- The expertise and capabilities that the partner brings to the project

- The time saved by Air Products in reaching project goals
- The net R&D dollars saved
- Access to background intellectual property (IP) of the partner
- The intellectual property expected to be generated by the project

The final two characteristics for each project are "impact parameters." Each of these parameters receives extra weight, using a scale of one through five.

One impact parameter is a financial impact (or commercial impact) rating. The highest score (five) goes to a project that will generate more than $50 million in annual sales, or more than $7 million in annual savings, or enables an entirely new business. A somewhat lower score (three) is assigned to projects that are expected to return $10 million to $50 million of annual sales, $1 million to $7 million of annual savings, or result in a new product line or major process change. The next level down, or a score of two, identifies projects with $1 million to $10 million of sales, or between $100,000 to $1 million of savings, or a new single product or an incremental process improvement. A score of one is reserved for projects that are expected to bring in less than $1 million of sales or only $100,000 of savings.

The final impact parameter in Figure 11-1 is technical leverage. The highest score goes to a "blockbuster," with lower scores for projects expected to deliver a major advance, an incremental improvement, or a straightforward improvement.

Results from Forty-Two Projects

By evaluating the project ratings as well as the averages and medians, Air Products and Chemicals determined that the average project saves hundreds of thousands of dollars of net R&D cost. For the portfolio of forty-two projects, Air Products is probably saving at least $4 million, and possibly a great deal more than that in net R&D effort. The story is similar for time savings, with the average project saving about two years. The evaluation shows that the forty-two projects are collectively saving more than 80 person-years of effort.

The commercial impact measure is not as straightforward, since annual sales growth or other cost savings occur only if the project, and all of its related activities, are successful. However, there is no reason to expect that Air Products' probability of success in external projects will be any different from its internal projects. Some percentage of the forty-two projects will deliver tens of millions of dollars of commercial impact.

By leveraging Air Products' internal projects portfolio with its external programs, the company is producing a significant return. By measuring the success and impact of the external technology development program, senior management has information to guide their investment decisions, improve the portfolio of external projects and drive the mix to higher average values. The goal is to successfully leverage R&D resources to attract more important and higher-payout programs into the external research effort and improve the overall return from technology development.

Share this rating tool with top management and ask for their reaction. Pilot it on some of your current projects and compare its value to the measurement system you currently use. The best way to assess the value of a tool is to use it.

Air Products and Chemicals' metrics are designed to assess the value of an external relationship. While value is a critical aspect of success, there are other aspects of alliances that lend themselves to measurement and improvement as well. In the next section, we will show how Eli Lilly and Company and Procter & Gamble Pharmaceuticals measure other aspects of alliance performance.

Alliance Implementation Metrics and Alliance Improvement

An alliance management system must include metrics to measure implementation success and enhance interpartner communications. Good metrics tell a story. They identify the factors that are important in the alliance and follow them over time. Good metrics are actionable. They guide line management's thinking on tactical changes, which help managers achieve goals. Good metrics rely on easy-to-verify information that is readily available. Poor metrics, by comparison, require information that's difficult to find and subject to bias and interpretation.

For example, if the alliance has readily identifiable goals and objectives, the metrics jump out at you. Revenues are a clearly applicable metric in a co-marketing alliance. Cost of goods sold is a useful metric in a manufacturing alliance. However, most alliances are multicomponent. They often include an R&D component as well as marketing, sales, physical distribution, and customer service components. Performance of some components is easy to measure. Performance on others is difficult to assess. Alliance success also depends on soft measures such as communication effectiveness and the personal drive of individuals. Multiple components lead to the need for multiple metrics. The metrics are dynamic, evolving to match the changing needs and objectives of the alliance.

Metrics are of little use unless they are coupled to methods for improving performance. The best alliance measurement systems are part of larger systems for ongoing improvement. Let's look at two excellent examples, from Eli Lilly and Company and Procter & Gamble Pharmaceuticals.

Eli Lilly and Company's Alliance Management System

If decoding the weak signals of early-stage alliance distress is an art form, then Nelson Sims is the new Picasso. As head of the Office of Alliance Management at Eli Lilly and Company, he leads a group of alliance managers who play a crucial role in Lilly's success. One manager from Sims's group is assigned to every alliance in Lilly's portfolio. That person's bonus is 100 percent tied to the success of the alliances under his or her care. Success is defined as an alliance reaching its goals, not just Lilly's success in reaching its own corporate objectives.

You get what you reward in organizations. If you don't reward it, you won't get it.

Through years of experience, Lilly has systematized its approach into the Lilly Alliance Management Process

(LAMP) program.[2] Part of the program is to train people from both Lilly and each of its partners in the best practices of alliance management. Part of the program is to help assess the health of every alliance on a regular basis. LAMP managers have the responsibility for using appropriate planning, organizing, and join-up processes, as well as fixing alliances if they get into trouble.

Some failure is expected in a business as complex and risky as pharmaceutical drug development. The path from experimental compound to commercial success is intended to be a fine filter allowing only the most safe and efficacious drugs to reach the marketplace. However, many alliances fail not because of technical difficulties, such as drug safety or effectiveness. They fail because of relationship diffculties, such as unlinked decision-making structures and unresolved conflict. A review of Lilly's past alliance history showed that the company was better than average in most attributes that make a good partner, but the company needed to improve in order to lead the industry. A basic pattern emerged that suggested Lilly's alliance success resulted from the ability and determination of motivated individuals on both sides, rather than from any kind of systematic management process. For example, during the early stages of finding partners and consummating deals, considerations about whether the parties could actually work together were rarely considered, or they were treated as secondary to the primary objective of meeting project milestones. It seemed that Lilly might have been lucky rather than proficient at alliance management. Does this sound familiar?

Except for the fact that the LAMP program is focused on alliances, the concept is not new. Firms have used sophisticated change management systems to deal with environmental issues, reengineering efforts, Six

Sigma quality initiatives, and ISO certification. If Lilly management was going to significantly impact shareholder value through alliances, they needed to systematize their approach. That meant training managers, creating procedures, and assessing success along a set of predetermined criteria, all with the goal of making Lilly the best alliance partner in their industry.

The biggest responsibility of the Office of Alliance Management (OAM) in any alliance is to act as the advocate of the alliance, rather than represent one or the other partner. This ombudsman role was a new one in Lilly and had to be carefully explained to people both inside and outside the OAM. Determining the responsibilities of the ombudsman was another important task. One role is to lead partners through the complexity of Lilly's organization. Lilly is a multinational pharmaceutical company with more than 35,000 employees. Even sophisticated partners need help navigating through Lilly and getting things done.

To deal with these issues, every alliance has its own three-person management team responsible for the relationship's success. The team includes an alliance champion, an alliance leader, and an alliance manager. These three roles in Lilly's system are roughly equivalent to the typical roles (described in Chapter 9) of the Alliance Executive, Operating Manager, and Support Specialist.

The alliance champion is usually a top executive who is responsible for the overall support of the relationship. That person's responsibility is to facilitate communication between Lilly and the partner, and to break down any bureaucratic barriers that impede progress.

The alliance leader is usually a technical manager, a project leader, or other senior person with an intimate knowledge of the alliance focus. This person is the day-to-day leader of Lilly's side of the alliance and is accountable for the overall success of the alliance.

The alliance manager represents the OAM. This person's primary responsibility is to support the alliance leader and act as an advocate of the alliance. The alliance manager is trained in alliance tools, metrics, and management techniques. As the primary business integrator, the alliance manager is available to help the Lilly alliance leader and the partner resolve differences, provide training, and serve as chief diagnostician in assessing the health of the alliance. The responsibilities and degree of involvement of the alliance manager vary from alliance to alliance. The alliance manager is always available for consultation and facilitation. However, the alliance manager may not always be directly involved in the daily activities of the collaboration.

To determine the level of OAM involvement in any particular alliance, Lilly assesses its 140 relationships along two dimensions: strategic importance and management complexity. Alliance managers are more deeply and regularly involved with alliances of higher strategic importance and higher complexity.

The key to OAM's success is the quality of its people. Lilly's alliance managers are experienced professionals with a wide range of functional backgrounds. Marketing managers join forces with technical Ph.D.s, who easily mingle with finance and corporate affairs experts. Managers are assigned to the alliances that best suit their background, and each manager is in constant contact with the others for help and support. To ensure the knowledge created in one alliance is transferred to the rest, this group meets every Thursday morning to share experiences and work out difficult issues. If an alliance is in distress, its alliance manager describes the situation and leads a discussion on possible resolution strategies. The output from this discussion is fed back to the alliance leader and alliance champion for implementation.

The Alliance Health Survey

Lilly's Alliance Health Survey is used to check the health of every alliance on a regular basis. This Web-based questionnaire covers fourteen distinct dimensions identified by Lilly managers as key indicators of success for their alliances. Since the fourteen dimensions are applicable to all of Lilly's alliances, the survey can be used to compare one alliance with another, or track a single alliance over time.

Figure 11-2 compares the results of two alliances. Alliance A shows significant signs of distress while Alliance B appears to be in good health. The overall assessment of Alliance A is only fair (average favorable ratings of 60–70 percent), with significant differences in the assessments of the partners. Using the information from the Alliance Health Survey, the alliance leader and alliance manager worked with the partner to review such matters as task assignments and specific goals. Some people on both sides were reassigned. Six months later, the collaboration was much more productive and the interfirm relationships were much healthier.

Alliance B required no intervention. However, the results were shared with the partner, emphasizing the importance of the quality of the relationship.

The Alliance Health Survey is just one example of an alliance management tool. There are many others, including widely published team-building exercises such as Best Friend and Mission Impossible, and proprietary Lilly instruments such as the "strategic futures" tool. These tools are all part of an alliance management program that is managed and organized using software known as the Partners' database. The Partners' database ties the entire program together. Its purpose is to systematically capture, codify, and share what alliance managers learn about partnering skills. The Partners' database contains information about all of Lilly's alliances, including a high-level overview, the collaboration's contract, governance agreements, meeting minutes, lessons learned, milestones, budget reporting, as well as existing tools, processes, and instructions for how to use them.

How effective is the program? Lilly senior management is convinced that the company has become a more partner-friendly organization, and the annual Alliance Health Survey shows that Lilly has significantly improved its ability to diagnose and resolve difficulties in its alliances. Partners are calling the Office of Alliance Management and asking for assistance. The most telling measurement, though, is the competitive response. At least three major pharmaceutical companies are creating their own version of Lilly's program. Becoming the "Partner of Choice" is the pharmaceutical industry's new mantra. The goal is to build competitive advantage by using organizational magnetism to draw the best new technology and compounds into the firm's drug development and marketing pipeline. The magnet's power is tied to the firm's alliance management capability.

Procter & Gamble's Alliance Effectiveness Assessment Survey

Tom Finn and Dave McCamey are the lead alliance experts for P&G's Pharmaceutical (P&GP) division. Each played an active role in P&GP's alliance with Aventis, which led to the commercialization of the osteoporosis drug Actonel. Each is a coach and mentor for P&GP alliance Operating Managers and Implementation Team members. Using their experience in what makes alliances

Figure 11-2. Eli Lilly and Company's Alliance Health Survey.

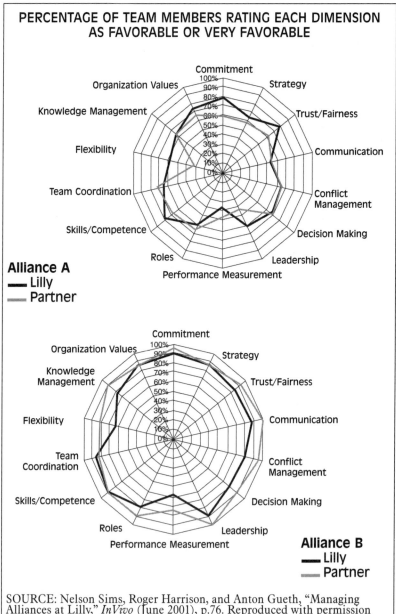

PERCENTAGE OF TEAM MEMBERS RATING EACH DIMENSION
AS FAVORABLE OR VERY FAVORABLE

SOURCE: Nelson Sims, Roger Harrison, and Anton Gueth, "Managing
Alliances at Lilly," *InVivo* (June 2001), p.76. Reproduced with permission
from Windhover Information, Inc. Copyright (2003) Windhover
Information, Inc. All rights reserved.

work, they developed an implementation assessment tool that focuses attention on key elements of success. That tool, the Procter & Gamble Alliance Effectiveness Assessment survey, is designed to assist alliance Operating Managers and Implementation Teams in monitoring and improving the performance of their alliances.[3]

Like most companies in the pharmaceutical industry, P&GP cannot internally develop all of the technologies needed for marketplace success. They are increasingly dependent on the ability to create and manage alliances. To meet the challenge, P&GP management asked Finn and McCamey to study the factors that lead to alliance implementation success.

By combining the experiences of P&GP managers with the insights of leading alliance experts, Finn and McCamey developed the Alliance Effectiveness Assessment survey. The tool is used by the Implementation Teams of both P&GP and its partners to identify implementation weaknesses and to drive action to improve performance. Equally important is the survey's ease of use. P&G took its expertise in maximizing customer satisfaction and built it into the alliance tool. The result is a survey that is short, right to the point, and very useful. Each question focuses on a specific implementation area while simultaneously leading the user toward changes that improve performance. The nine areas measured by the tool are:

1. Senior Management Commitment
2. Right People and Resources
3. Aligned Direction and Plans
4. Clear Responsibilities and Expectations
5. Robust Communication

6. Effective Decision Making

7. Disciplined Improvement Approach

8. Aligned Work Systems

9. Constructive Conflict Resolution

The best way to understand the survey tool is to use it. For example, the need to deal with systems alignment became painfully clear during one of P&GP's most important alliances. A seemingly minor incompatibility in the partners' e-mail systems almost caused the collapse of the relationship. The incompatibility led to e-mail messages arriving very late. When a person's counterpart in the partner firm received an e-mail message and responded, the response often went to e-mail heaven. Tensions grew quickly as people assumed their counterparts were ignoring their requests for information, input, feedback, and meeting times.

Select your most prominent alliance and answer the Aligned Work Systems question in Figure 11-3. How did your firm score?

That experience led to the development of the Aligned Work Systems question (Figure 11-3). While the question highlights issues and suggests solutions, it is accompanied by a set of coaching points that lead managers on both sides through a structured thought process to reach a mutually agreed-on solution. The question is scored on a scale of zero through eight, with eight being the highest score. Managers are encouraged to regularly monitor the health of their alliance and use the tool to suggest improvements.

Figure 11-3. Alliance Effectiveness Assessment: Aligned Work Systems question and coaching points.

How effective are your work systems in your alliance? Assign a score on a scale of 1-8, where:

0= Little or no work has been done to identify or align key work systems or methods that must be in place to support the alliance. People must constantly struggle to overcome system incompatibilities to get alliance work done

4= Some basic, key work systems are aligned (e.g., e-mail). However, other important systems or methods are still separate and cause delays and rework, because neither side is willing to compromise on their internal approach.

8= All key work systems and methods are fully integrated with demonstrated performance sufficent to meet alliance needs. People are able to work with their partners as if they were in their own company.

Examples of work systems or methods are: e-mail, forecasting, business tracking, safety data tracking, technical data access, national sales meetings, budgeting, quality assurance standard operating procedures, and regulatory report formats.

Aligned Work Systems Coaching Points

Purpose of the Coaching Points: The goal is to reach a score of 8, where all essential work systems and methods are fully integrated with performance sufficient to meet alliance needs. People are able to work with their partners as if they were in their own company.

Coaching Points

1. Think broadly when considering what "systems" need to be aligned (i.e., not just IT or manufacturing systems). Consider all management processes that are used to move ideas, money, projects, materials, and otherwise support decisions. Examples: e-mail, forecasting, business tracking, safety data tracking, technical data access, approach to national sales meetings, budgeting, quality assurance standard operating procedures, regulatory report formats.

2. Plan and budget for this work. Identify the systems that need to be aligned, the capability of adapting the systems, and the cost of doing so (e.g., in terms of the money, time, personnel commmitment, time taken from other internal work, the cost of adding personnel to align the systems, etc.). Once it is known what alignment needs, costs, and commitments have been made, establish a realistic timetable with a buffer.

3. Involve IT and finance early in alliance work plans. They need lead time to build systems bridges. Don't assume IT people will "make it happen" overnight—these folks are often left out of the loop.

4. Prioritize the systems needs based on the expected workflow. Start with communication systems, key software, then specific work systems. Don't make people jump through extra hoops to communicate across an alliance or they won't do it. Be thorough in the analysis and prioritization of systems to be aligned.

5. Resolve incompatibility. Have each party explain the systems that they routinely use to do this type of work. Consider adopting the system from one of the parties before considering a "bridge" between the two systems.

6. Anticipate and share each party's plan for changes or major installations of infrastructure components (e.g., e-business software). Provide enough lead time so that each firm can plan their response to the coming change. When necessary, seek to isolate the alliance from otherwise corporatewide systems changes if they will seriously disrupt work and communication.

7. Communicate progress on system alignment and train people in the resulting changes.

The tool asks managers to explore important details rather than focusing on high-level concepts.

Finn and McCamey suggest that Implementation Team members work on one or two high-impact, doable changes that emerge from the Alliance Effectiveness Assessment survey. After agreeing on the key areas for improvement, team members from P&GP and the partner develop action plans to improve performance both immediately and in the long term. One person from each partner is assigned as co-leader to implement the change.

Beyond the Alliance Effectiveness Assessment survey, P&GP provides significant additional alliance implementation support. A P&GP Alliance Guide is published to present additional suggestions and details to Implementation Teams. One senior executive from P&GP and another from the partner firm have oversight responsibility for each alliance. Those leaders have sufficient authority to command resources from other P&GP and partner organizations. P&GP also invests in training for alliance managers. For example, one manager attended an eight-week training course on "Working with People from Different Cultures" in preparation for an assignment as alliance Operating Manager. To clarify individual roles and responsibilities, P&GP uses the Expectation Mapping tool (discussed in Chapter 9) to coordinate the activities of functional pairs. Communication, both within P&GP and with the partner firm, is facilitated by "town meetings" where employees are asked to join management for an update. Other communication tools include monthly reports, e-mails, Implementation Team Web sites, and video- and teleconferencing presentations.

Alliances also benefit from dedicated staff support. Finance managers from both firms meet to develop a common understanding of matters such as mechanisms for the flow of funds between the partners. They must also learn to speak with one financial "voice" to Implementation Team members from both sides. To facilitate implementation planning, all key managers from both firms meet for one week to clearly define priorities, issues, and strategic plans for the next eighteen months.

Measuring the Unwanted

There is nothing worse than measuring what you think is important, but isn't. A major chemical company measured itself on growth and linked executive bonuses to that measure. This company began acquiring companies and adding product lines. However, profitability suffered because of poor post-acquisition integration, the premium paid over earnings, and a focus on growth rather than on profitable growth.

The same company changed its metric and is now measuring profitability. Managers are suffering from organizational whiplash as they shed the assets they just acquired in order to reduce costs, overhead, and personnel. The emphasis moved from acquiring companies to divesting assets. The new corporate goal is to acquire individual products, technologies, and distribution channels through alliances. Make sure you are measuring the right things or you will be rewarding the wrong behaviors.

———

Be careful what you measure, because you will get it . . . and it may be unwanted.

———

Tips for Managing the Alliance and Determining Metrics

When setting up a management system and determining metrics, remember to:

- Address each of the eight characteristics of an effective alliance management system.
- Tailor the system and reporting requirements to the needs of your organization. One-size-fits-all systems have limited value.
- Choose metrics that are actionable, guide employee behavior, and are composed of easy-to-verify information that's readily available. Good metrics tell the story of your project.

- Determine what behaviors the metrics are likely to engender in employees—remember, you get what you measure in organizations.
- Tie metrics to performance appraisals for maximum effect.
- Share your alliance metrics with your partners. If you are setting up metrics for a particular alliance, jointly develop them with the partner.

Notes

1. The information in the section on Air Products and Chemicals is excerpted from Merrill S. Brenner and John C. Tao, "You Can Measure External Research Programs," in *Research★Technology Management* (May-June 2001), pp. 14–17. We would like to thank Dr. Tao, Mr. Brenner, Air Products and Chemicals, Inc., and *Research★Technology Management* for permission to present this information.
2. Nelson Sims, Roger Harrison, and Anton Gueth, "Managing Alliances at Lilly," *In Vivo* (June 2001), pp. 71–77.
3. Tom Finn and David McCamey, "P&G's Guide to Successful Partnerships," *Pharmaceutical Executive* (January 2002), pp.54–60.

C H A P T E R   1 2

MANAGING CULTURAL DIFFERENCES

Managing cultural differences is a major dilemma during the implementation phase of an alliance. Since culture isn't something that you can see, and few executives understand it, culture is an aspect of alliances that few manage. This is not to say that managers do not have an opinion on the topic. They do. Some books on alliances talk about the need for the partners' to assess each other's culture to ensure cultural fit. Others discuss the need to understand the partner's culture and to "integrate" the cultures during implementation. What these books fail to tell you is what "culture" is and how to deal with it. Without an understanding of these fundamental concepts, making a cultural intervention is out of the question.

Take that thought one step further. Have you ever

been trained to manage culture? What corporate resources can you call on to help you integrate cultures? How much time did you spend managing culture in your organization last week? If your answers to all three questions are "never" or "none," how can you cope with cultural issues in an alliance?

Given all the hoopla surrounding culture, it is not surprising that many managers consider the need to integrate cultures central to the success of the alliance. However, even professionals cannot agree on a definition of culture. Kroeber & Kluckorn are two anthropologists who searched the literature for definitions of culture in fields as diverse as art and psychology. After finding 300 different and sometimes conflicting definitions, they gave up.[1] We will not enter into the definitional debate here. Rather, we will use a commonly accepted definition in the management field and focus our attention on the practical steps managers can take to deal with culture in alliances.

What Is Culture in an Organizational Context?

Culture is shared knowledge embodied in the values, beliefs, and norms used by members of the organization to carry out their day-to-day tasks. It can be thought of as "taken-for-granted assumptions" about how to perceive, think, and feel about the events within a department or an entire firm. It provides meaning and predictability in daily affairs based on the knowledge of "how we do things here." Culture provides powerful yet unspoken directions on what is important and how things get done. These messages shape people's behavior.

Cultural norms are pervasive and shared among people from the executive offices to the mailroom. In the old Bell Laboratories, the "not invented here" (NIH) syndrome was widespread. NIH was a norm driven from the top and shared by people who otherwise differed in their tastes, dress, and personal style. Why is culture important? It explains the behavior of people, and behavior is what alliance implementation is all about.

Developing a sense of culture means that you have to put on an anthropologist's hat and look around. What do the offices look like? How are people dressed? What kinds of pictures and jokes are on the walls? What are the taboos? Observing the natives in their natural habitat is an important form of cultural learning. Employees of IBM do things differently from employees of Yahoo! The "ties vs. tees" are not right or wrong; they are simply different, and correct for each corporation's culture.

Managers working on alliances often describe culture slightly differently. One described culture as the 800-pound invisible gorilla quietly tearing away at the fabric of the alliance. Another manager described his firm's culture in the following way: "We're like the Klingons around here. Once we don't need you, we shoot you and push you out the spaceship door." He went on to say, "Once I went to my boss and said that I was going to negotiate a win-win alliance. He told me that in this company, win-win means we kick their butts twice!" It should come as no surprise that this firm's track record on alliances is dismal.

Absent an alliance, managers don't spend much time worrying about culture. They don't have to. Working on internal projects and interacting with people embedded in the same organizational culture facilitates goal achievement. People know what to expect from one another and can predict how individuals and groups will react to common situations. Add an alliance partner to the equation and things change.

Alliances bring culture out of the shadows and highlight the differences between firms. It is difficult to predict the behavior of the partner's employees. Actions and meanings that are taken for granted in your firm can surprise the partner. One large firm clearly understood that its growth strategy required alliances to meet corporate objectives. Their first few alliances were successful but unnecessarily painful. Sensing that culture was somewhat to blame, one executive interviewed alliance Operating Managers in his firm and in the partner firm. Arrogance was a word he heard often from partner employees. They complained of poor collaborative skills, limited employee empowerment, and inflexible midlevel managers. Constant personnel turnover and rigid corporate processes further interfered with relationship building. One manager at the partner firm summed up his feelings this way: "In our company, people are encouraged to take risks and we can fail honorably. In your firm failure is not an option. We encourage revolutionaries, you shoot them." These were not easy messages to hear or bring back to the organization, but the comments from the partners were consistent with the views of the firm's own alliance Operating Managers.

Based on many years of success in developing breakthrough products, this firm had established a culture of "no one does it better than us." The processes, systems, and management attitudes that embodied that success were institutionalized into the organization. People were rewarded for behaving and thinking like their bosses. Successful employees "fit in" and followed the accepted ways of doing things. As long as the organization focused on internal projects, the systems worked well. When a partner was added to the mix, the knee-jerk reaction was to fix the partner and institutionalize "our" systems in "them" as well.

What can alliance Operating Managers do? How can they deal with cultural differences while maintaining their focus on accomplishing the goals of the alliance? The answer can be thought of as a continuum anchored at both extremes. At one extreme, alliance Operating Managers can deliberately ignore culture and hope for the best. At the other extreme, they can systematically characterize the partner firms' cultures, evaluate those characteristics for compatibility, and actively manage the resolution of cultural differences where those differences threaten the success of the alliance. Firms tend not to be at either extreme.[2] Instead, most firms use an ad hoc approach for integrating cultures.

The ad hoc approach relies heavily on top management and stems from the belief that executives lead the culture creation process by actively and regularly communicating their values, beliefs, and expected behaviors to the Implementation Teams. Sometimes alliance Operating Managers from both firms get together and agree on a set of behaviors that they will encourage in the alliance. Most times they do not. Rather, the norms of each firm independently guide that firm's Implementation Team behavior. Alliance Operating Managers hope that synergy, not conflict, will result from the meeting of the cultures.

There is another reason alliance Operating Managers and Implementation Team members are skeptical about using tools to manage culture. Many corporate employees have been "culturally managed" in their own careers. They have learned the difference between what executives say they expect and the executive's own behaviors. Top-down-directed behavior in an alliance is adopted only if the leaders visibly display the values they preach. Adoption is further reinforced when the new norms are included in performance evaluations, training programs, and the overall reward system.

In our experience, no alliance has ever undertaken a formal, large-scale cultural intervention, defined as a systematic attempt to create a productive culture in the alliance or successfully integrate the cultures as they currently exist. Nor do we recommend the idea. Large-scale cultural integration efforts are best viewed as a special case of change management. Companies spend years of effort and millions of dollars implementing Six Sigma programs, quality initiatives, and reengineering their organizations. In each case, success requires top management commitment, a sustained effort including substantial resources, and continual training at all levels of the organization. A true cultural integration program is at least as difficult as these more traditional change management efforts. We do not know of a single executive who was willing to undertake that level of effort during an alliance. Nor do we think it necessary.

Given the complexity of culture and its interdependence with other organizational constructs such as structure, power, and centralized versus decentralized decision making, the best path forward is for firms to deal with culture by applying management techniques that are more powerful than culture, and that are under management's control. To understand how these techniques are more powerful than corporate culture, we must examine the three types of culture.

Three Types of Culture

It is easy to overstate the uniformity of culture within a firm. For example, the R&D and marketing organizations of a firm will have many similarities rooted in the firm's values but some differences in their norms and collective behaviors.

Cultural differences come in three flavors. There is national culture (Japan vs. the United States), corporate culture (IBM vs. Merck), and subunit culture (marketing vs. R&D). Some forms of culture are relatively strong, meaning that they exert their influence on people's actions in obvious and predictable ways. Others are relatively weak, in that they are less important in influencing behavior. In general, national and subunit cultures are stronger and corporate culture is relatively weak. An example will clarify the issue.

Companies such as IBM and Merck deal with all three types of culture simultaneously. Each firm has employees from many nations. Each firm has a corporate culture, and each firm has a variety of subunits with their own definition of "how we do things here."

Figure 12-1 highlights the distinction between corporate and subunit culture. Both IBM and Merck have an R&D organization with scientists and engineers steeped in the traditions of exploration and discovery. Each firm also has a sales/marketing organization with experts able to understand a customer's needs and create appropriate solutions. However, even though IBM's R&D and marketing departments are in the same firm, they resemble their respective groups in Merck more than they do each other. Trivializing these differences is a mistake. Cultural leverage points and barriers emerge from this bubbling stew of values, beliefs, and behaviors. The "way

Figure 12-1. Distinction between corporate and subunit culture.

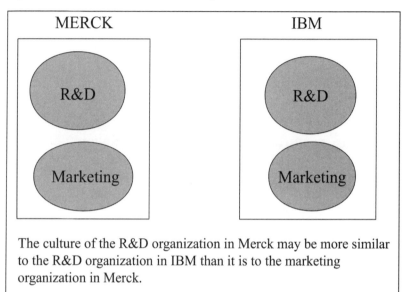

MERCK   IBM

R&D   R&D

Marketing   Marketing

The culture of the R&D organization in Merck may be more similar to the R&D organization in IBM than it is to the marketing organization in Merck.

we do things here" thinking emerges from all three types of culture.

The value of understanding the three types of culture is that alliance Operating Managers can make a rough prediction of whether culture will be a problem in the alliance. Figure 12-2 compares two difference alliances. The first is a collaborative R&D relationship between two U.S. firms. The second is a product development, manufacturing, and marketing agreement between a U.S.-based start-up and a very large firm based in Japan. It is less likely that culture will interfere with the performance in the U.S./U.S. alliance because the firms share the same national and subunit cultures. The only difference is corporate culture. Not so with the U.S./Japanese alliance. Since all three types of culture are different, there is an increased likelihood of cultural distress. This simple analysis also highlights the areas where cultural intervention may pay the highest dividends. In most cases, alliance Operating Managers should emphasize sensitivity training around the stronger national and subunit cultures while paying less attention to the weaker corporate culture.

Figure 12-2. Impact of the three types of culture.

	Alliance #1	Alliance # 2
Type of Culture	Collaborative R&D between U.S. firms	Product development, manufacturing, and marketing between a U.S. and Japanese firm
National	Same	Different
Corporate	Different	Different
Subunit	Same	Different

The Impact of Personality and Language on Culture

Ready to manage culture yet? Well, hold on. Two other factors affect culture and can be mistaken for it: an individual's personality and language barriers. It's best to start with the individual's personality.

Personality and Stereotype Traps

In the early 1990s, the Industrial Research Institute (IRI) conducted a study of success factors in international joint ventures. The goal was to interview managers in cross-cultural relationships between companies in the United States and Japan, the United States and Germany, and the United States and the United Kingdom to determine the factors that lead to success. The stereotypical behaviors of each national culture quickly emerged during the interviews: "United States managers are cowboys. They shoot from the hip and ask questions later." "The Japanese are consensus driven." "The Germans are exceptionally well organized."

However, during every interview another concept emerged and dominated the conversation. Managers who began the discussion describing stereotypical behaviors quickly added, "My counterpart is not like that." These managers understood at a subconscious level that while stereotypical behaviors attempt to describe people as a group, their daily interactions were with a counterpart who was very much an individual. Since individuals can show radically different behaviors from those displayed by the group, the stereotypes were meaningless.

Stereotypes are created in people's minds from an array of sources: family biases, the media, and the person's casual contacts with a few individuals who fit the stereotypical behavior. Human nature being what it is, stereotypical descriptions are often negative.

The interviews revealed that managers quickly moved past their preconceived stereotypes of people in other cultures when they began to work with their individual counterparts. They attributed success (or lack of success) in cooperative work to their counterpart's personal characteristics, such as reliability, respect for another's views, and the ability to work together across geographical and organizational boundaries. The IRI study showed that stereotypes are misleading when dealing with individuals.

Figure 12-3 explores this concept in more detail. The broad bands in Figure 12-3 represent stereotypical behaviors of the German culture, as perceived by the IRI interviewees. The stereotypical German is organized and formal. However, the IRI respondents characterized their own German counterparts at various places inside each broad band. German manager A is disorganized and very formal at work. German manager B is organized but not very formal.

The point is that trying to manage cultural integration as a group phenomenon is a mistake. The IRI interviews showed that each German manager was a unique individual whose personality was a far better predictor of his behavior than national culture. At one extreme, some people are pleasant and easy to work with. They can't help

Figure 12-3. Bands of behavior.

	Organization	Formality	
High	Manager B	Manager A	Stereotypical German managers score high on both dimensions.
Low	Manager A	Manager B	

Managers A and B show different patterns of behavior relative to the stereotype of German managers.

it, and their culture doesn't require it. They're just nice. There are people at the other extreme as well. These vast differences in behavior have nothing to do with culture. However, they are attributed to culture when people don't know other individuals well enough to place them into the category of "nice" or "jerk."

Language Traps

Business people have communicated across language barriers since the dawn of civilization. Language barriers create a variety of traps that interfere with accurate communication. Some of these language traps are particularly important when an executive is trying to manage an alliance.

We will focus on the common, but not universal, situation where the partners agree that English will be the primary language in the alliance. Americans and other native English speakers often find that many of their foreign counterparts appear to communicate well in English. While allowing for the need to translate documents and use interpreters with those people whose English ability is clearly limited, the native English speakers (and their English-speaking counterparts) assume that language issues are under control. That assumption creates two traps for the unwary.

The first trap is that the use of a foreign language shapes a person's behavior. Try this experiment. Take your spouse to a Mexican restaurant and use your high school Spanish to discuss the menu with the waiter. Count the number of times you are asked to repeat a word because of your incomprehensible accent. Feel your body tense up as you try to ask about a specific dish. Experience the sense of relief when you switch back to

English and are able to communicate again. That is the situation many non–native English speakers deal with every day in an alliance, even if their English ability is much better than your high school Spanish.

Years ago, an American negotiator learned about the impact of language on behavior while negotiating a joint venture agreement with English-speaking Spanish executives. The negotiations were conducted in English without the use of interpreters. The American negotiator found one of the Spanish negotiators especially difficult to work with. The individual's somewhat sour disposition and negative personality often got in the way of progress. After negotiations were successfully completed, the American firm sent a native Spanish-speaking executive to Spain to be the managing director of the newly established joint venture. Much to the American negotiator's amazement, the managing director reported that the so-called difficult Spaniard was a highly positive and cheerful person when speaking his native language. He was easy to work with, but only in Spanish.

The second trap is that nominal fluency can mask subtle but vital differences in the meaning of English words and those same words in another language. Alliance negotiations and implementation often deal with complex issues that are discussed using words with subtle meanings. Both the native English speaker and the person who learned English as a foreign language may not realize that they have a different understanding of an issue based on their different interpretation of the same word. A misunderstanding based on language subtleties can remain hidden long after the damage is done. At that point, one partner may accuse the other of deliberate deception, not realizing that the trouble arose because of the different interpretation of a word's meaning.

People on both sides of an international alliance can minimize the negative impacts of the two traps by recognizing them and taking appropriate actions. For example, awareness that apparent fluency in English may mask subtle differences in meaning should lead the native English speaker to speak clearly and deliberately, avoiding the use of idioms. The non–native English speaker should ask for clarification when an English phrase is not understood. Both sides must recognize that a highly skilled interpreter should be used in difficult negotiations, even if it appears on the surface that interpreters are unnecessary. These actions require sensitivity and courtesy on both sides to avoid the appearance of insulting people who may pride themselves on their English-speaking ability, and who may be perfectly able to communicate in English in less complex social conversations.

Transmitting Information, Listening, and Displaying Patience

Poor speaking, writing, and listening skills create communication errors. Some errors stem from simply not knowing the other person. Others stem from language gaps and cultural differences. These errors are particularly troublesome during alliance negotiations and in the early days of implementation when people are still getting to know one another. For example, when two people know each other well, they exchange a great deal of information through their tone of voice, body language, and facial expressions. When a close personal relationship does not exist, a familiarity gap is created that affects communications. This familiarity gap is found in both international alliances and alliances between firms from the same nation. Part of the solution involves recognizing the problem on both sides. The rest of the solution can be summarized in one word: patience.

When delivering information, both sides must be aware of the pitfalls of using verbal shorthand in describing alliance ideas, even if a skilled interpreter faithfully translates the verbal shorthand. Charts, pictures, and carefully written text should be exchanged and thoroughly discussed to be sure that both sides understand each other. Both sides must pay attention to body language and the tone of the communication as well as the translated words. All of that is not going to happen if the partners try to rush through an alliance discussion in a few hours. That is particularly true if one side has just flown across seven time zones. A common mistake among executives is not devoting the time and energy needed to develop an interpersonal bridge across the familiarity gap.

Face-to-Face vs. E-Mail

In today's world of e-mail and videoconferencing, it is easy to over-rely on technology to communicate. While these communication tools add value, they also introduce an increased risk of miscommunication in alliances, especially in early stages of implementation when people do not know each other well. As a general rule, interteam communications should be face-to-face during the early days of an alliance. Personal contact allows Implementation Team members to build the interpersonal relationships important to the smooth functioning of the alliance. Once interpersonal relationships are established, tools such as videoconferencing and alliance-specific Web sites can be used to supplement ongoing face-to-face meetings. Quarterly meetings are natural face-to-face meeting points. They are regularly scheduled, occur at appropriate intervals, and include recreational as well as formal events.

Alliance Operating Managers and Implementation Team members must be careful not to deliver bad news or discuss difficult issues over the phone or by e-mail. The increased possibilities of miscommunication compound the problem as people begin to project what they believe are the other side's motivations into the message. The larger the gap between the intended and received communication, the larger the possibility that the communication will worsen the problem, not solve it.

Workable Strategies for Dealing with Culture

With limited resources and competing demands on people's time, we suggest that firms carry out a few simple but powerful cultural interventions. Depending on circumstances, those interventions may be done with Planning and Negotiating Teams during negotiations or with Implementation Team members and other alliance participants during implementation. We suggest several ways to overcome cultural barriers while simultaneously focusing team members' attention on the goal and objectives of the alliance.

Knowledge

The first step in dealing with cultural barriers is to identify the dominant behaviors people are likely to observe in their counterparts. In international relationships, firms use cultural training courses to learn about the cultural norms of the partner. For example, the American firm in a United States/Japanese alliance should take its Planning and Negotiating Team through a training program in which members learn about Japanese personal and business customs. Before starting to implement an alliance with an Argentinean company, an Implementation Team might learn about the political, economic, and cultural history of both Argentina and its regional neighbors. Properly focused training programs led by experienced people can overcome many misleading prior assumptions about national stereotypes and provide insights into both the diversity and unifying threads of the national culture. More important, well-planned training programs help participants understand the specific cultural differences that affect alliance formation and implementation.

The behaviors that emerge from corporate and subunit culture are best learned through a pen-and-paper cultural inventory, a standard tool in organizational development. Easy to administer and score, these inventories do a good job of identifying dominant behaviors in firms or in subunits inside firms.

Here's how a cultural inventory could be used at the start of alliance implementation. Team members from both partners score typical behaviors inside their firm using the same set of relevant parameters, such as "attitude toward competitors" or "willingness to accept ideas from outside the firm." Scores for both firms are provided to all members of both Implementation Teams. In that way, all alliance participants have insights into their own firm's likely relevant behaviors and the behaviors of the other firm.

As with any organizational behavior tool, these results must be used with discretion and a small dose of humor. In our example, both Implementation Teams could be asked to predict what alliance activities might cause interpartner conflict, based on the results of the shared pen-and-pencil inventories. In an informal setting, Implementation Team members can discuss the aspects of culture that might get in the way. After such interfirm discussion of dominant behaviors, an alliance Operating Manager in the middle of a dispute may be able to identify the role of cultural differences in the dispute.

Trust and Respect

The development of interpersonal trust and respect is a powerful force in organizations. A cultural intervention program can provide Implementation Team members with ways to get to know one another as people and professionals. Activities that foster personal bonding help bridge cultural gaps. Some of these activities are natural aspects of alliance implementation. However, both firms must be conscious of the positive effects of bridging cultural gaps using activities designed to encourage people to develop a closer personal understanding of each other. Examples are technical visits between people working on joint projects, joint presentations of project results, or interfirm planning sessions. The goal is to break down isolation and build interpersonal respect through careful planning and execution of joint functions.

The experience of two California electronics companies describes the power of interpersonal trust and respect. The activities of this large company/small company alliance included cooperative research, manufacturing, and distribution. During the early days of implementation, the alliance was having more than its share of growing pains, including miscommunications, poor project coordination, and interpersonal conflicts among key people. One day, an earthquake seriously damaged the large company's facilities. Their executives called the small firm's top management and asked if the large firm's scientists and engineers could work temporarily in the small company's facility while the large firm's laboratories were being repaired. The answer was, "Send them down." The temporary assignment to the small firm's facility led to three unexpected outcomes. The goals of the alliance were achieved ahead of schedule. Four new areas for joint work were agreed upon. And the large firm's scientists and engineers didn't want to go back. How were the start-up difficulties transformed into cooperative success? Working-level people had the opportunity to get to know one another at an interpersonal level. They got to know, trust, and like each other.

Cultural differences cannot stand up under a relentless assault of trust and respect.

Communication in alliances is really a dialogue of actions, not words. When people from both firms have a chance to work closely together, their actions speak volumes about their intent, competence, quality of character, and caring.

Team Building in Alliances

We are not enthusiastic advocates of expensive and time-consuming exercises in team building, such as white water rafting and swinging through trees. However, there are less elaborate ways to break down barriers that are fun, inexpensive, and achieve the critical results of allowing people to build interpersonal relationships.

Communication in alliances is a dialogue of actions

Here are a few simple team-building tools we recommend:

- *Go Bowling.* That's right, go bowling. Bowling is the perfect sport for team building because most people are terrible bowlers. We all look dumb in those rented shoes, and you can bowl with a beer in your hand. The bowling teams must be arranged carefully. Company A team members never compete against Company B team members. Rather, the functional pairs identified in the Expectation Mapping process pair up and compete against other functional pairs. Think of it as a cultural intervention with the perfect disguise. People have fun while building interpersonal relationships. Bowling works well in both same-nation and international alliances.

- *The Culturally Correct Dinner.* Food and fun are a powerful combination. If the partner firms are from different nations, the culturally correct dinner is an interesting way to break down cultural barriers. Here's how it works in a United States/Japanese alliance: The U.S. Implementation Team invites their Japanese counterparts into one of the U.S. team member's home for dinner. The hosts prepare their Japanese counterparts a traditional . . . Japanese dinner. Listen to the howls of laughter as both sides try to eat this concoction. Then, turn the living room into a karaoke bar. Every moment the people from the partner firms discuss food, culture, and traditions they are building stronger interpersonal relationships.

● *Secret Weapon People.* Once alliance Operating Managers recognize that alliances are relationships between people as well as companies, they tap into a hidden reservoir of power in their firm; secret weapons that convert cultural barriers into bridges. The most powerful weapon is the simple attraction of one person to the goodwill of another. Cultural differences disintegrate when confronted by someone who has an unusual curiosity about another's culture. You know the type. These people go on vacation to interesting places and gleefully immerse themselves in the culture of the host country. Rather than sitting on tour buses, they wander around the marketplaces, enjoy the local foods, and talk to the people they meet. At night, these people build instant cultural bridges as they try to sing the native songs and dance the traditional dances. Place one or two of these "secret weapon people" on the Implementation Team and watch them glue the firms together with smiles and warm feelings.

Tips on Managing Culture

Alliance managers cannot ignore the concept of culture, yet few managers make a proactive attempt to manage it because they do not know how. In our experience, there are three factors that are more powerful than culture and that are under the control of management. Managers can form interpersonal bridges that are more powerful than cultural barriers by actively encouraging team members to:

- Understand the dominant behaviors in each firm's culture.
- Develop trust and respect between counterparts.
- Have fun together.

Notes

1. A. Kroeber and C. Kluckorn, Culture: *A Critical Review of the Concepts* (New York: Vintage Books, 1952).
2. Gene Slowinski and Matthew W. Sagal et al., "After the Acquisition: Managing Paranoid People in Schizophrenic Organizations," *Research*Technology Management* (May-June 2002), pp. 21–31. Although this study focused on post M&A integration, our experiences on the management of culture in alliances is similar.

C O N C L U S I O N

Two factors conspire to generate the 70 percent failure rate of alliances. The first is that many failed alliances should have never been formed in the first place. Alliance is the latest business buzzword. This leads inexperienced executives to create too many relationships or alliances that do not benefit from the strategic and operational planning needed for success. We do not believe in forming large numbers of alliances. Rather, we believe that firms succeed by creating a few very strategic alliances tightly linked to the strategies of both partners. Once those alliances succeed, the firm can take the learnings and expand its portfolio into other areas of strategic interest.

The second factor is a lack of business development experience in one or both companies related to alliances. The purpose of this book is to fill that gap with tools, metrics, and management techniques that leading companies use to create their alliances. However, words in a book are not sufficient to prepare managers for the complexities of inter-organizational relationships. Once again, we encourage managers to use this book in cooperation with experienced legal and business development professionals who can tailor the principles we describe to the firm's unique situation.

Although the focus of our book is on relationships between firms, you may wonder if it is possible for profitable alliances to occur within the corporation. How can business units work together more effectively to meet customer needs? What are the possibilities for new markets and technologies if intrafirm alliances become the norm? After we gave a major presentation on alliances, the chief technology officer of a *Fortune* 500 firm raised his hand and said, "You don't know anything about alliances. What you know how to do is cross an organizational boundary. It is irrelevant if that boundary is internal or external!" We agree. The principles outlined in this book allow managers to cross the no-man's-land of organizational boundaries no matter where those boundaries lie. Look internally as well as externally for opportunities to create value.

The benefits of alliances are not limited to the for-profit sector. These relationships have a great deal to contribute to the nonprofit and governmental sectors of the economy as well. The potential for economic development is significant when inner-city entrepreneurs and community-based organizations look at alliances as a strategy for delivering high-quality goods and services. One example is the joint venture between Pathmark Corporation and New Community Corporation (NCC) in Newark, New Jersey. NCC is a nonprofit social services organization created after the 1967 riots. Following the riots, many businesses left Newark, including all of the grocery stores. Inner-city residents had to travel great distances or pay high prices at local bodegas for their grocery needs. NCC believed that a major grocery store would succeed in Newark, and it acquired a site on which to build a store. However, no one at NCC had the skills to manage the complex operations of a modern grocery store. To overcome that weakness, NCC formed a joint venture with Pathmark to build and manage a grocery store in Newark.

NCC's contribution included the site and its ability to work with inner-city community members. Pathmark brought its expertise in grocery store management. The success of that store is legendary. After many years of operation, it is still in the top 20 percent of stores in the Pathmark chain. This is one example of how the not-for-profit sector can achieve its objectives using sophisticated business models like alliances.

Finally, the logical conclusion of the increased use of alliances is a network structure of the organization. If alliance creation and management becomes a core competency of multiple firms in the same industry, the power of the entire network will emerge. Leading companies in the pharmaceutical and electronics industries are quickly moving to that model by combining the strengths of leading companies and focusing them on a specific set of objectives. By putting together a "Dream Team" of alliance partners, the network is able to maximize its probability of success while spreading the risk among partners.

None of this is possible without a laserlike focus on the fundamental principles outlined in this book. When executives get the fundamentals right, the rest follows.

Good luck!

INDEX

281

For more information on the
Alliance Management Group, visit online at
www.strategicalliance.com.